MOMMIE'S BRIGHT SUNSHINE

Moving Beyond the Death of a Child
While Grieving a Future Not to Be

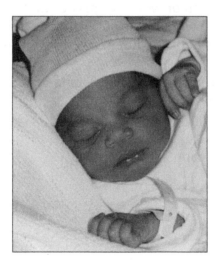

TONYA M. LOGAN

PRESS

Support for years.
Thank you for being my friend!
TM Logan
2/2/14

Mommie's Bright Sunshine
Moving Beyond the Death of a Child While Grieving a Future Not to Be
by Tonya M. Logan

Printed in the United States of America

ISBN 9781628713336

Unless otherwise indicated, Bible quotations are taken from the King James Version of the Bible.

www.xulonpress.com

TABLE OF CONTENTS

INTRODUCTION

As is true of most little girls, we have a fantasy of how our life will turn out. We will move out on our own as soon as we can to break away from the rules because rarely do we think our parents understand us. We will choose the perfect white dress and as we walk down the aisle to meet our prince charming, all eyes will be on us. We will have a boy and a girl and probably a dog. After making a great deal of money and having a significant impact on the world, we will retire and travel the world with our husband as our children will be successful, professional, and independent.

The world has a way of working out differently than we could ever imagine.

I began this story one day before my 31st birthday: March 28, 1997. My 30th year was so traumatic that I suppose I felt the need to regain some semblance of control. I had no preconceived notions as to how this book would turn out—whether it would be a book to be sold or a documentation for myself—but it is an honest account of how I recall the details of the injury and death of my beloved daughter, Kayla, and how the grace of God pulled, and continues to pull, me through life's challenges. I wanted to document accurately before I forgot or before I was called to join Kayla. I did not want to miss the opportunity to share my life -changing (and, in many ways, life -enhancing) experience with others. Following such a great tragedy, two things can happen: either you become embittered by the loss or your heart gets immeasurably bigger. In any case, no one is left unchanged. On the other hand, the question begs... is it that we are really changed or simply different from who we thought we were and what we believed we were to become? Since God knows the beginning from the end, my future is laid out differently from what I would have chosen. I feel this story is important because not only am I a part of the group whose heart has gotten immeasurably bigger, but also because my faith is unquestionably much stronger.

I jokingly told my therapist at the time that I might write a book because I have not done things according to the "textbook." It is usually said that you should not make major decisions within six months of a significant loss. I made several. Within one month of my daughter's death, I interviewed for a new job (which I subsequently accepted) and I constantly pressed my husband of two years to leave our home. The therapist agreed that I should write a book. She remembered that Kayla was with me during my session the very day prior to the accident. The point I make is that you must do what is right for you and not according to any "textbook." You will discern what that is with God's help. I certainly do not want people to feel sorry for me because I am truly and undoubtedly blessed. Although I have had to find a way to live without Kayla's physical presence, I have accepted that I am "parenting a memory" as coined by Elizabeth Edwards following the death of her son, Wade. I want people to "fill in the blank" and know that God can, and will, take care of all things if you have the discipline to ask, wait, and then fully trust only in Him—and not ourselves.

DEDICATION

This book is dedicated to all of the bereaved parents regardless of how this unimaginable loss has occurred. I pray that God will bring you the comfort and peace that He has so mercifully granted me all of these years. Our God is an awesome God!

In addition, I have to dedicate this book to my parents, Leonard and Betty Maiden, as they have helped me to parent my two blessings God has brought into my life, Haven and Christian. I have always said, *"I may be a single parent, but I am not parenting them alone."* My parents are the two who have helped me to grow to see the truth in one of my affirmations.

Lastly, Janet Oro came into my life in 1993. First colleagues, now sisters. Janet comforts me non-judgmentally and without unsolicited advice. What a gift! I practically owe my life to Janet—my sister born to different parents.

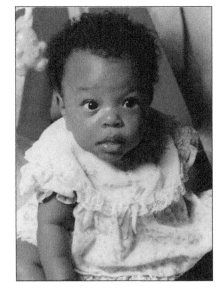

ACKNOWLEDGMENTS

The late Dr. Phyllis Galloway was a church member at the time I began drafting this book. She was the first to read the manuscript and share her insight. Phyllis continues to be on my mind although she is rejoicing with Kayla.

Patrice Heinz and I met when we crossed paths professionally in 1994. Our friendship has deepened tremendously. Pat was extremely non-judgmental when my anger was expressed toward Kayla's father. She is certainly a phenomenally inspirational woman.

Diane Banks became my supervisor in 1996. We, too, have continually developed a very meaningful relationship although I left that agency in 1999. Diane has a unique perspective on this book because at the time she read it, she was not a bereaved parent. Sadly, her daughter Kia, died unexpectedly on May 26, 2004. Diane and I are able to connect with one another as only bereaved mothers can.

Harvey Schweitzer and Shane Salter met with me privately to discuss the process they experienced in getting their books published. They helped me to see that with perseverance and determination, it CAN get done.

Aaron Munson, who connected me with Xulon Press Publishing, and Tracy Ruffin both did editing. It was helpful to incorporate their ideas and suggestions as they approached this project with their own style.

At Xulon Press Publishing, Jack Walton (Publishing Consultant) maintained contact with me for many years and even prayed with me over the phone during a particularly difficult period in my life. He helped me to contact Jose Medina (Primary Account Representative) of Xulon Press Publishing so that this book could be moved into its final stages.

Lastly, this blessing would not have been birthed without the professionalism of Jason Flecher (Book Sales Representative) and Terry Haines (Marketing Coach) as well.

Justin Baskerville helped me to get some information that I needed as part of this book which saved me a great deal of time. He might feel he was simply "doing his job," but I am well aware that not everyone does their job and certainly not well or as professionally as he.

Again, thank you to all who had an impact in this enormous undertaking and prayed for its success. I offer thanksgiving in advance to those who support this endeavor and will continually pray for God's favor in the life of me, my family, and this book.

> *O My Father, if it be possible, let this cup pass from Me: nevertheless not as I will, but as Thou wilt."*
>
> *Matthew 26:39*

THAT FATEFUL DAY

*"Being a full time mother is one of the highest salaried jobs...
since the payment is pure love." ~Mildred B. Vermont*

With uncertainty taking place in my life, one thing was certain – my daughter was the one constant joy for me. As cliché at it may sound, Kayla was the light of my life. One of my greatest desires was to be a mother, and God graciously granted me that opportunity.

On the morning of September 4, 1996, the alarm went off at 4:45 a.m. I was tired and stayed in bed with Kayla for about another half hour. Coincidentally, it happened to be my second wedding anniversary, yet my husband and I had been sleeping in separate bedrooms for about two months. Just before that, we had been separated for about a week, but it was very important to me that Kayla had a relationship with her father. I decided to let him return.

Because I was nursing, I had Kayla sleep with me even though doctors discouraged this because of emotional and physical hazards. I remember looking at Kayla and thinking how beautiful she was and how happy I was with her, although other parts of my life were unraveling at the seams.

This particular morning started out like any other. I was due to be at my job, For Love of Children (FLOC), by 7:00 a.m. Each morning, the first thing I would do is pump my milk. Then, I would nurse Kayla because she was always able to get out what she needed even after pumping. I prepared her bottles, fed her rice cereal and fruit, and got us ready to leave.

Finally, I got up and started my daily routine. I called the babysitter at about 6:30 a.m. to let her know I was running a little late. My husband gave me a lovely plant and card for our anniversary. I was surprised, but pleased, and I even took that plant to my office. Kayla and I arrived at the babysitter's house, and I put the food and bottles in the refrigerator as was my normal routine. I said goodbye, but regrettably, cannot remember kissing Kayla goodbye that morning.

A week prior, I recall thinking, on at least two occasions, that I should call the babysitter and tell her to check on Kayla. These thoughts always occurred around noon. I stopped myself from calling because I did not want her to think I was a nervous, overly cautious, new mother. I reassured myself that all was well and there was no need to fear. In retrospect, I should have followed my maternal instincts, but I truly believe God was preparing me for what would happen days later.

It was close to two in the afternoon, when I heard my name being paged by the receptionist. She stated that I needed to call the front desk immediately. Unfortunately, I was on the telephone and unable to accept the incoming call from my mother. I eventually ended my call thinking that it was probably some worrisome foster parent, as I was often paged, although there usually was no real emergency. How I now wish that was the case. When I finally was able to respond to the page, I was surprised to find my mother on the line. I knew immediately something was wrong. There was great distress in her voice. All I could hear her say was, *"You need to give the nurse some information so that they can admit Kayla to the hospital."* Incredulous, I said, *"What happened?,"* but she was crying and handed the phone to the nurse. Of course, I knew something was terribly wrong, since my mother was unable to speak or give me any information when I asked, but I never fathomed what was yet to come.

I went into absolute panic mode. I had already started trembling as I spoke to the nurse. Somehow, I forgot the name of the organization where I worked and my address and telephone numbers, but it surprised even me that I was able to recall both social security numbers of Kayla and myself. How odd! Now frantic, the tears exposed the depths of my nervousness, uncertainty, and shear fear. After I looked at my business card and provided the nurse with my work address and telephone number, I was able to ask the nurse, *"What happened?"* She told me that Kayla had fallen off the bed. Instantly, I began thinking, *"Well, what is the big deal about that? Don't most children fall off the bed at some point? She was probably taken to the hospital just as a precaution, or maybe she needed a few stitches, then she could go home. My mother always overreacts so that is probably why she could not respond to me."* These thoughts were temporarily reassuring. At the time, it never occurred to me that my mother was already at the hospital or why the babysitter had not called me herself.

I could see the office parking lot from my office window. Another car had blocked me in because parking was definitely at a premium. I was still crying when I asked one of the secretaries to locate the person blocking my car because I needed to leave immediately. I also asked her to call my husband and tell him to meet us at the hospital. I had already called him and discovered that he had left work early because he was not feeling well, but had yet to arrive home. I did not want to leave a message on the answering machine because he did not check it very often, and I wanted him to hear the information firsthand. My supervisor was working with another social worker at the time. I burst into her closed office to interrupt them. I mustered enough strength through tears to blurt out, *"I do not know what happened to Kayla, but she's in the emergency room. I will call you later."* She asked me if I needed any help, and I said, *"No,"* before rushing out to my car.

There was torrential rain that day, almost blinding. I later learned that September had disproportionately more rain that year than in any other month. It seemed as if it had all decided to come down within that particular week. I was driving erratically I am sure and trying to think of how to reach the hospital. I have absolutely no sense of direction and usually do not mind getting lost, but there was no time for that this day. I was desperately trying to get there as quickly as possible, and I was afraid I would not choose the shortest route because I certainly was not thinking clearly. I could not imagine how to get to the hospital at that point. By God's divine intervention, I somehow found myself on Michigan Avenue. The car was practically driving independently of me as I was praying and not paying much attention to my driving. Just imagine the overwhelming sense of panic of a mother on her way to the hospital after receiving an alarming call about the welfare of her child.

At His touch, my faith grew instantly, and I learned what it meant to totally trust in God and to be open to listening to Him.

I recall driving in the left lane because I can remember thinking that I needed to make a left turn to get onto Twelfth Street. Unfortunately, I discovered that I could not make a left turn there, but had to make a right turn and then a left to get to where I needed to be. I was a ball of confusion, and the street signs were of no help. Additionally, the rain had not let up one iota. I looked up into my rearview mirror and saw there was no traffic, and, thankfully, I could get over easily. That moment is frozen in time for I had been praying, *"God let me get there in time; don't let me have an accident, and let my baby be okay."* While still looking into my rearview mirror, I felt the hand of God or one of His angels touch me on my left shoulder and all of the anxiety instantaneously drained my body—from head to toe. I have come to realize that fear and anxiety are incompatible with God, and they are washed away when we surrender our heart and cares to Him. I also believe that must have been the moment that God knew that this was certainly more than I could handle because He gave me His immediate and undivided attention. I do

I have come to accept that fear and anxiety are incompatible with God. They are washed away when we surrender our heart and cares to Him.

not recall verbally asking for His presence, but spiritually, my heart must have made that fervent plea. I knew that I needed God's grace and mercy, but I had so many other things that I was concentrating and not concentrating on at the time. Now, I do not think that I consciously turned my situation over to God. Rather, at the moment when I needed it most, He chose to take my burden upon Himself, and for that I am eternally grateful. God's divine intervention allowed me to accept what was happening and to have peace that truly surpasses understanding regarding Kayla's situation. When I felt the hand of God physically touch me, I knew that everything was going to be alright. This special moment with God reminded of the scripture, 2 Corinthians 12:9, that says, *"And he said unto me, My grace is suffi-cient for thee: for my strength is made perfect in weakness. Most gladly therefore will I rather glory in my infirmities, that the power of Christ may rest upon me."*

It seemed like an eternity, but I finally arrived at the hospital. *"If only I could now find a parking space,"* I thought to myself. I was so close, yet so far away. I parked on the street because I had no money, did not know how long we would be there, and did not feel like fighting with parking attendants. I later learned the parking at the hospital was free, but I never considered that possibility. I went to a locked door near the emergency room. The ambulance drivers were still outside as I had arrived within about twenty minutes of my mother's telephone call. They asked who I was, and I said, *"I'm Tonya Anthony. Kayla's mother."* One of the paramedics whisked me inside and said, *"This is the mother."* Now, I am thinking, *"Why do they know me? Why do I stand out?"* Later, of course, I realized that this was another clue or sign that the situation was very grave and that Kayla would be leaving me.

Upon arriving at the hospital, I learned that when Kayla was found at the babysitter's house, she had no pulse and was in both cardiac and respiratory arrest. CPR was being performed until the paramedics took over and medications were administered. Although weak, Kayla's pulse was restored, but she was unable to breathe on her own and her heartbeat was excessively fast once she arrived at the hospital. I was informed that there was no spontaneous movement and her pupils were mid-position, dilated, and fixed. Before I could get to the waiting area to talk to the doctors and to see my

> *"It might be our loss, but God's gain."*
> *~Russ Parr*

mother, the first person I saw was the hospital chaplain. He was standing outside the door to the waiting room. His presence struck me as strange, which caused my thoughts to race. *"Why did they call the chaplain? Kayla only fell off the bed. Don't all babies fall off the bed?"* In retrospect, this was yet another clue God was giving me that she was leaving her earthly vessel.

My mother and the babysitter were crying almost uncontrollably. The babysitter said she tried to call me at work, but I was on the telephone. She did not think to have me paged, but called my mother, as an emergency contact, instead. By the time my mother got to her house, the ambulance had already taken Kayla and the babysitter to the hospital.

I was not able to see Kayla immediately because she was still being evaluated. The chaplain asked if Kayla had been baptized which both alarmed and annoyed me because it seemed like an inappropriate question at the moment. I replied, *"Yes, July 21."* Little by little, God was letting me become aware, but it was hard to comprehend or even think in those terms. God had compassion and did not overwhelm me, but rather allowed the gravity of the situation to sink in slowly. The babysitter hugged me and kept apologizing for what happened. I said, *"It's okay. God has already told me that she is going to be alright."* She looked at me in total disbelief. She said that she would continue to pray for Kayla and send up points of light.

I called back to my office and learned that my husband had been reached and was on his way to the hospital. I shared with them that Kayla was on life support and would later learn that the office had several prayer sessions for us. I called a friend whom Kayla and I were supposed to visit that day to meet her three-week-old son and explained the situation to her. She prayed with me over the telephone and said that she would continue to do so.

A very nice nurse was talking to us and checking with the doctors to find out when we would be able to see Kayla. The head pediatrician was still evaluating her. Finally, we were able to see Kayla. When I first saw my precious child, I did not need the experience of a medical school education to immediately internalize the gravity of the situation. She was hooked up to so many tubes, her eyes were closed, she did not move at all, and her color did not seem quite right. Kayla only had on a diaper, and I was thinking how beautiful she had looked that morning in her new dress. *"And where were her shoes I had just bought her that weekend?"* No, my thinking was not at all rational, but I suppose it was my mind's way of protecting me from the inevitable. A short time later, my husband arrived just as I went in to see Kayla. My father got there moments later. I was shocked to see my father was crying! *"How could that be? Nothing ever bothers him."* Of course, I knew that he loved Kayla with all his heart, but to actually see my father's pain was very, very difficult for me. We were all so empty at that point that we seemingly had nothing left to give and definitely nothing to give to another person. There was a simultaneous and overwhelming sense of feeling exhausted, depleted, and helpless to say the least. Both my husband and my father were so distraught, I remember thinking, *"What have they been told because they could not possibly know the worst of it?"*

We were all crying, but I attempted to get all the information I could. Once a social worker, always a social worker. More importantly, I was a mother trying to protect my child so I tried desperately to grasp what was

God bears our burdens when they are too much for us.

happening to my baby. I can still vividly recall the words of the pediatrician, *"Should she survive, she will have considerable brain damage."* There is certainly no gentle way to tell a mother that her child is going to die. I was thinking, *"SHOULD she survive? Is there a possibility that she may not survive?"* That morning, Kayla was going to college (preferably my alma mater, the University of Virginia) and by that afternoon, our world had been turned upside down. My mind jumped ahead—as it frequently does—and I began thinking of all the things that would need to be done to care for her properly, like moving her frequently to prevent bed sores, since the doctors had given no hope for Kayla's full recovery. The doctors had said Kayla would most likely be on a feeding tube and a respirator. I am one that always tries to face reality, but the enormity of this reality was certainly a very bitter pill to swallow.

Always needing to be in the middle of everything, I looked on Kayla's chart and saw that they had my baby's name spelled, "Rayla." I quickly informed the nurse, who was happy to be helpful to us in some small way. Of course, I understood that the priority was stabilizing Kayla and not completing paperwork, but I had chosen such a beautiful name for my child that I wanted it to be right. At least it gave me something else to focus on momentarily.

One of the nurses later said that they had to cut Kayla's dress off of her, which was inconsequential to me. Still, she had looked absolutely beautiful that day. Kayla had been wearing a white blouse with a dress that went over it and tied on the sides. I think the dress had a yellow flower embroidered at the neck. She had on green, orange, and yellow sandals with a lion on them that I had just purchased on our trip to Durham, North Carolina, while visiting my cousin and Kayla's godmother the previous weekend. In hindsight, I wish that I had gotten that beautiful dress back from the nurse, even if it was cut into shreds. I feel as though it is another part of Kayla—the last thing she touched—that I could held onto.

I left the emergency room so that I could get out of the way, but I had also had enough to digest at that point. I touched my baby, but she did not respond to me. *"Did my baby even know I was there?"* I went into the hall and a nurse followed me out. I told her it was my second anniversary, and she thoughtfully said, *"Happy Anniversary."* I

In hindsight, I wish that I had gotten that beautiful dress back from the nurse, even if it was cut into shreds. I feel as though it is another part of Kayla; the last thing she touched, that I could hold onto.

remember that I wore my black and yellow tiger print outfit with heels to work that day. I rarely dress up and was thinking, *"Of all days for me to dress up. It's pouring down rain, and I may be sitting at the hospital for hours.*" My thoughts were filled with such inconsequential things, but I knew it was only a temporary diversion.

The nurse said, *"You do not need to be strong at a time like this."* I assured her that I knew that, but as a friend, Leatrice Burphy, once said, *"You never know how strong you are until being strong is the only choice you have."* What I did not say was that God had so clearly spoken to me earlier. Since we were at a Catholic hospital, I knew that my openness about my spirituality would be welcomed. It was apparent that either Kayla would be healed on Earth and be the child I dropped off that morning, or she would be healed in Heaven. My mind and spirit simply could not grasp the doctor saying that Kayla would have considerable brain damage *"should she survive."* As Christians, we are taught to acknowledge God's will, and there are times in most people's lives when we must accept God's will over ours. Even Jesus was not exempt from this when He prayed in the Garden of Gethsemane to have the cup that lay before Him to pass him by. Yet, He humbled Himself and accepted God's will over His own. This experience with Kayla is the first time that I can say that I was accepting of God's will even though it was directly in contrast to mine. I was able to seek guidance and wisdom from God and recognize where my responsibility ended and His began. It says in Ecclesiastes, *"The race is not to the swift nor the battle to the strong."* Thank God the battle is not mine, but His. I later read in Acts of Faith by Iyanla Vanzant, *"When a prayer is answered, there is no need to cry."* I had prayed for Kayla before her birth, every day after her birth, and, of course, after her injury. I prayed that if she was not going to be my vibrant, responsive child, then she would be healed in Heaven so that neither she, nor I, would suffer. Of course, the outcome was not one I would have hoped for, but it was one that with God's help I would able to live with.

God's Boxes
by Arielle Perkins

I have in my hands two boxes
which God gave me to hold.
He said,
"Put all your sorrows in the
black, and all your joys in the gold."
I heeded His words, and in the two boxes,
Both my joys and sorrows I stored.
Though the gold became heavier
than the day before.
And the black was as light as air.
Curious, I had to open the black one,
I wanted to find out why.
Then I saw in the base of that box a hole
my sorrows had fallen out by.

I showed the hole to God, and mused aloud,
"I wonder where my sorrows could be."
He smiled a gentle smile at me.
"My child, they're all here with Me."
I asked, "God, why give me the boxes,
Why the gold and the black with the hole?"
"My child, the gold is for you to count
your blessings, the black is for you to let go."

THE SECOND HOSPITAL

"Look for the face of God in the winter of discontent as well as in the summer of joy. He is the God for all seasons."
~Thomas Nelson

I was told that Kayla would need to be transported to Children's Hospital. At first, I was told I could ride in the ambulance with her, but soon after, that plan was scrapped. I saw my baby on the stretcher just prior to her being put into the ambulance and thought, *"Look how small she seems among all these adults, equipment, and tubes."* Through it all, never once did she move any of her extremities.

We arrived at Children's Hospital about 5:30 p.m. I had to go to the Admissions Department and try to reach her pediatrician's office. I had been having tremendous problems with the insurance company at the first hospital and did not feel like hassling with them yet again. The pediatrician was reached, and the insurance company gave authorization for the emergency admission. I went back upstairs to the Pediatric Intensive Care Unit to wait. We could not see Kayla right away because her vital signs were not stable. I began thinking, *"God please don't let her die before I have a chance to say goodbye."*

During this waiting period, I called my supervisor because she had left a message on my home answering machine. When I spoke to her, she said, *"Tonya, I got really scared when you were not home."* I told her that it did not look good. I was able to give her my appointments for the week because I did not know when I would return to work. At that point, no one indicated that Kayla was likely to die, but I knew even if she returned home, it would take a great deal of time for me to work out the details of her care, whatever that might be.

After I talked to my supervisor, I called one of my foster parents who happened to be a pediatric nurse. She was not at her desk and did not answer her page. There were few cell phones at that time. I called her at home and her husband said she had not gotten home, but asked was there anything he could do. Regrettably, I said, *"No."* I ended the call without giving him any details of what was happening. I tried the foster parent at work again. Miraculously, she answered that time. Through uncontrollable tears, I asked her to explain what the doctors were saying in a way that I could understand. I trusted her and felt that the doctors probably saw me as a lay person who would not comprehend medical terminology. She immediately began to cry, too, and said that I understood everything. Then, she asked me if there was anything she could do. Not wanting to burden anyone, I again said, *"No."* Unselfishly, the foster parent came to the hospital anyway and stayed for many hours. She brought snacks, a notebook, pens, toothbrush and toothpaste, disposable razors and shaving cream, a small back pack, and only God knows what else. Her presence there really helped, and it was also reassuring to me that the hospital was indeed, respecting me fully and explaining things to me very honestly and simply. Since this foster parent had worked at Children's Hospital previously, it seemed like the hospital staff respected that, too.

There was another set of foster parents who happened also to work at Children's Hospital. The husband worked in the emergency room and his wife on the burn unit. They worked different shifts, so one of them was always available to check on us. This is evidence that the Lord strategically places His angels wherever they are needed. These foster parents brought us drinks, pillows, and blankets. They even visited Kayla and spent time with us. Again, I thank God for designating such significant and helpful people to be instrumental at a time when I needed them most. It is nothing short of a miracle that I knew so many "inside" people. God surrounded me with people who were clinically knowledgeable and whose warmth and care made all the difference during one of the most difficult times in my life. I remember feeling safe in spite of the situation. Psalm 23:1-6 and Psalm 27: 1, 5, and 14 say, respectively,

> The Lord is my shepherd; I shall not want.
> He maketh me to lie down in green pastures: he leadeth me beside the still waters.
> He restoreth my soul: he leadeth me in the paths of righteousness for his name's sake.
> Yea, though I walk through the valley of the shadow of death, I will fear no evil: for thou art with me; thy rod and thy staff they comfort me.
> Thou preparest a table before me in the presence of mine enemies: thou anointest my head with oil; my cup runneth over.
> Surely goodness and mercy shall follow me all the days of my life: and I will dwell in the house of the Lord forever.
> The Lord is my light and my salvation; whom shall I fear? The Lord is the strength of my life; of whom shall I be afraid?
> For in the time of trouble he shall hide me in his pavilion: in the secret of his tabernacle shall he hide me; he shall set me up upon a rock.
> Wait on the Lord: be of good courage, and he shall strengthen thine heart: wait, I say, on the Lord.

Finally, we were able to see Kayla. Again, she was so still. Looking at my baby, it was gradually becoming obvious that she was going to leave me. The doctors said that Kayla did not have very much brain activity. I said, *"It looks like she is trying to breathe on her own because sometimes she looks as though she is holding her breathe while other times it looks as though she is gasping for air."* A nurse said, *"Yes, she is breathing on her own somewhat because the respirator causes breaths to be very regular, but breathing is one of the most basic functions of the brain."* I later learned that Kayla's pupils would sometimes dilate, which is also another very basic brain function.

Unable to control her body temperature and having no cough or gag response, I was told that Kayla was not responding to deep pain. I took that to mean that she also was not experiencing any pain. I found that news very comforting because the doctors had so many things attached to her, and I did not want her final hours to be difficult ones. I asked another nurse if Kayla was crying because there appeared to be tears in the corners of her eyes. She said, *"No, that is called third spacing, and it is further proof that the brain is not functioning properly. There is fluid in the body, but the brain does not know where to send it so it pools wherever it can."* My husband chose to believe that Kayla was crying and saying, *"Please do not give up on me."* My mother added that perhaps she is crying and saying, *"Please let me go."* I accepted the nurse's explanation and did not believe she was crying as a way to communicate, but took it as further evidence that Kayla's brain cells were continually dying.

My husband and I went home for about an hour so that we could change clothes, feed the two dogs, and drop off one of the cars. I decided to pump my milk as well. Just as we got into the house, the telephone rang and it was Kayla's pediatrician. She arrived at Children's Hospital after her husband came home so he could be with their young son. She said that she would wait for us to return. We did what we needed to do, and I packed a few things – one being Kayla's <u>Children's Bible</u>. I also got some bottles because I needed to keep pumping my milk in case Kayla recovered and needed to nurse again. After getting some things together, we headed back to the hospital.

24

As soon as I got to the family conference room at the hospital, I saw one of my girlfriends from church. She came out and gave me a big, warm, much needed hug. We did not really say anything to one another, but she did say that she was so sorry. The assistant minister of my church, Trinity A.M.E. Zion, was also there. Kayla's accident happened to occur on a Wednesday, meaning the assistant minister and my girlfriend were together because they had gone to Bible study. After my cousin called the church and told them what happened, they dropped everything and came to support us. The three of us talked in the hallway. The assistant minister said, *"I am praying for Kayla's restoration."* I replied, *"That's fine, but should God decide to take her, it is okay with me."* She seemed somewhat surprised by this and said, *"You know He can do it."* I reiterated, *"Of course, but whatever decision He makes is okay with me."* The assistant minister went into the intensive care unit alone to pray over Kayla first and then asked the family to come in for a group prayer. She asked all of us to touch Kayla somewhere on her body. There were so many people around that bed—at least fifteen family members and friends. I was touched by the number that had rallied around us merely hours after her accident. I was at Kayla's head stroking her beautiful hair. Practically everyone was crying as we prayed for Kayla's restoration.

I was willing to accept God's will – even if it was different from mine.

Many of the family members and friends were understandably angry. After all, they had not had the encounter that I had experienced with God. Many people were saying such things as they "knew" we wanted to "wring the babysitter's neck" and advised us to be sure to have the incident investigated. Another person later said, *"What was she thinking? Of course five month olds are able to roll over!"*

The accident had happened so suddenly. Kayla had been put on an adult bed for her nap. She had rolled off the bed to the left, and her neck got caught in the legs of a wooden television tray placed beside the bed. Her oxygen was cut off for an indeterminate period of time. When the babysitter found her, Kayla was still hanging in the legs of the tray with her legs curved behind her. The babysitter's mother-in-law performed CPR while the babysitter called 911. When I think of what must have occurred that fateful day, I realize Kayla could have rolled to the right or at a different angle and would not have gotten hurt at all, but that is not how it all transpired. Her life on this Earth was to end that day and my belief is that it was simply meant to end in the way it did because if He had wanted, God could have prevented the accident from occurring.

While this event is most tragic and due to the work that I do, I thank God that Kayla was not molested, tortured, mutilated, or missing. She returned to her Heavenly home as perfectly as she had arrived. God knew it was important for me to say goodbye, so Kayla did not die before arriving at the hospital. I would be lying if I said that having the investigation and the skeletal survey did not help to ease any lingering doubts that may have crept in, but my attitude following her death has always been, *"Even if she [the babysitter] had done something to cause Kayla's accident, the end result would still be the same – Kayla would have died."*

My father went home that night, but my husband, his cousin, my mother, and I remained at Children's Hospital. The doctors said that if Kayla was going to recover, she would make remarkable progress within those next twenty-four hours. My husband and I slept on the cramped sofa while my mother slept in a chair and my husband's cousin slept in a recliner in a larger waiting room. She frequently came in to check on us, but I was somewhat dismayed when I over-heard her on the telephone telling someone that she was there for my husband. It really should not have come as a surprise because this cousin was often distant from me once she realized that I was going to be around. She and my husband were very close as they grew up together and were more like siblings than cousins. I suppose she felt displaced by our marriage in some way. Regardless, I was glad that she and several other relatives were there to support him because I was blessed to have the support of many tremendously caring people.

The next morning, Kayla had not made any progress, but rather, her condition worsened. She was no longer breathing on her own even intermittently, and her pupils were no longer dilating according to the "Brain Death Evaluation." The doctors told us that if Kayla failed the test a second time, they would be forced by law to turn off the life support within forty-eight hours. I had no idea of what to do at that point because I certainly did not want to be faced with the reality of ceasing the life support and then possibly regretting that enough had not been done. Could God give me a sign as to what was the "right" thing to do? Perhaps I could "bargain" with Him by agreeing to be a better Christian or gladly trading places with Kayla? Yes, those thoughts did fleetingly enter my mind, but as I was being the best Christian I knew how to be, what could I promise? If I was really going to trust God and do His will, I would have to accept whatever that might be even if it were not in line with mine. After thinking about the quality of life my child would endure by keeping her on life support, I was leaning toward making the decision to terminate the intervention that was keeping Kayla alive.

We remained at the hospital and visited with Kayla the entire day, holding her often. The doctor which would later be the one to cease the life support, helped me to position the tubes, while I held her in the rocking chair. Many people visited Kayla and held her that day. I am sure the nurses probably felt overworked, but there is no doubt how much she was loved.

The agency I worked for during this ordeal, For Love of Children, sent sandwiches and cookies to us in order to remind and encourage us to eat. It was so thoughtful because no one wanted to leave or to even think about eating. As a result, there was food and opened drinks remaining the following day. I remember my father asking if I wanted a fresh soda because the one I had was most likely flat. I mentioned to him that I was just going through the motions and not really able to taste or appreciate the food anyway. My supervisor brought us a dozen donuts. Somehow, all of the food was eaten by us, as well as the many family, friends, and visitors present which was a blessing because it was one less thing to have to consider and arrange.

After all of this, Child Protective Services (CPS) needed to interview my husband and me a second time despite us having already spoken to one of the hospital social worker's the previous evening. I told the investigator that I had no concerns about the babysitter, but I had not seen the room where Kayla had been sleeping. He knew I was a social worker, and he had worked with my agency previously. In some ways, I felt being a social worker gave me an understanding that may have been overwhelming to a lay person because I was well versed on the terms and understood the process that had to take place. I also think it helped others to see that I was still able to ask specific questions as I had done for years despite the tables now being turned.

During the second meeting with CPS, we were required to meet with a pediatrician who investigated child fatalities. When I saw her at the elevator, she began to introduce herself. I interrupted her and told her that I already knew her. She had been part of a Child Fatality Review for one of my cases about three months earlier. This pediatrician remembered me and instantly began crying. Actually, I was touched by her tears because her compassion was coming through and not merely her professionalism. She hugged me, and I knew she would be as helpful and gentle as she could while still conducting her interview. Even now, I marvel at how amazing and good God is. I could not have orchestrated a better team if that had been my intent.

We took the elevator upstairs to her office. I told the pediatrician that although the babysitter was unlicensed, a woman from my church and another social worker used that babysitter, although I had just met the social worker in January. Being licensed does not prevent traumatic events from occurring. I explained that I had made unannounced visits to introduce Kayla a few months after she was born and had even picked her up hours earlier than expected on several occasions to be sure that everything was as anticipated. My social work skills forced me to be cautious, and I had no concerns. Several people *Sometimes the best laid* had questioned why I chose to use an *plan are not enough.* unlicensed child care provider, but my husband and I interviewed both licensed and unlicensed providers and felt most comfortable with the one chosen. We also felt strongly that this babysitter had the best references of all those interviewed. I have never questioned my decision to utilize this person.

Again, I know this was part of God's plan. The babysitter had just started keeping Kayla about a month before the accident because I was on maternity leave for three months, my husband stayed home with her for one week, and my mother kept her for one month as part of my "transition plan." I wanted Kayla to gradually get used to being away from me. We completed the interview with CPS and returned to the family conference room downstairs.

To Me You are Special
author unknown

If God came down from Heaven
And offered me to choose
The greatest gift of all
I would only ask for you
If only I could touch your tiny fingers
And rub your tiny toes
To see your cute little smile
And touch your tender nose
Nothing could be more precious
Than the thoughts I have of you
To me you are still special
God must have thought so, too.

EXCITING POSSIBILITIES

"The lesson is to embrace your life, what happens to you, where it takes you and not fight it." ~Bill Warner

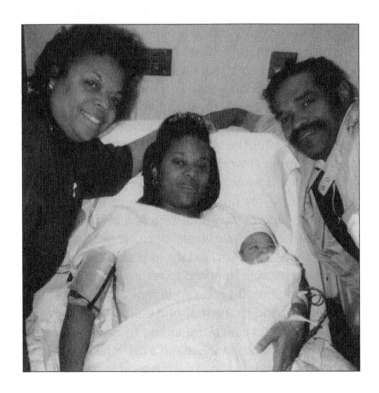

My husband and I married on September 4, 1994, after three years of dating. My mother, several of her friends, and I catered his grandparents' fiftieth wedding anniversary. We had met on September 21, 1991 at a church gathering, so I felt that this must have been "the one." We had a very difficult relationship, even from the very beginning, but, honestly, I was the one anxious to get married. I did not seek God in whether to marry this person, but rather figured that if God did not want this marriage to take place, He could certainly prevent it. Looking back, I think that what I really wanted was a beautiful wedding. I was not disappointed. Like most women, I envisioned this grand affair most of my life. I was twenty-eight years old and felt the time was right to settle down and start a family before my biological clock started deafening me. I did not really focus on the fact that once you had a wedding, you would then have to deal with marriage and all that it entails. Regardless, what I wanted even more than a fabulous wedding celebration was to have a baby. At that time, I was not secure enough within myself to have a child while unmarried—whether through adoption or birth.

As stated, the wedding was exceptional. It was the "perfect" day. Naively, I thought after the wedding ceremony that everything would be fine, as we had made a commitment before God and one another. The day after the wedding, we went to Maui, Hawaii, for two weeks. A former coworker arranged for us to stay at a property her parents owned as our wedding gift. The first ten days were wonderful. Initially, my husband had only wanted to stay for ten days as he said, "*I don't have that kind of leave,*" but he eventually agreed to stay the entire two weeks since we only had to pay for the plane tickets. I wanted to stay as long as possible because who knew when we would be able to afford to return. Surprisingly to me, my husband and I got into this huge argument on the eleventh day, and I took my ring off and threw it at him—along with some unsavory, non-Christian words. I called the airline to make arrangements to return home early, and my husband's dishonesty was exposed. I learned that the money I gave to my husband to pay the "balance" of the airline tickets was actually the total cost of the tickets although he had clearly said that was merely a fraction of the cost. During an argument about the cost of the tickets, my husband also said he mysteriously lost seven hundred dollars – seven one hundred dollar bills. That money was never found. I quickly began to question whether he ever had it, although I dutifully helped to go through the entire house and all of our belongings in an attempt to find the missing funds. Once I learned the penalty fee for changing the flight, I stayed in Maui for the remaining three days as I am known for my practicality. There was a tremendous amount of tension. What a way to start out a marriage! This time in Maui was the beginning of the breakdown of trust in my marriage. When I got home, I began to privately keep records of all of our transactions, which I stored outside of the house, and more was revealed to me. I will not elaborate on all the graphic details of our relationship as this is not a story about my marriage, but it provides background of the string of events that would soon take place.

After we married, my husband suddenly decided to join the military. This subject had not been previously discussed. He wanted to go to basic training for the Marine Reserves in October 1994, which was merely one month after we married. He knew that he would be gone for six months. I asked him to consider waiting until January 1995, so that we could spend our first holidays together – Thanksgiving, Christmas, and New Year's Day. Now that we were married, I had to sign all of the documentation for his enlistment, and I stubbornly refused. My husband was furious. We always had power struggles, and this was yet another one. Ironically, we argued on those three important dates: Thanksgiving, Christmas, and New Year's Day. Coincidental? I think not. Just as it was not coincidental that we argued on the eleventh day of our honeymoon, in my opinion, it was not by chance that we argued on those significant days either.

In January 1995, my husband left for the military. For the first three months, I could only write him. His mother called and asked if I missed him and I said, "*No.*" That truly caught her off guard, and she stopped calling. My husband's family never cared much for me, in my opinion, and was understandably happy when he returned from Basic Training. My family was so different from his. I believe that some of our problems were caused first by our differences in upbringing and second, by the instigation of his family. I am not saying that my family is perfect by any stretch of the imagination, but they did allow my husband and me to live our lives independently and make our own mistakes. Unfortunately, I cannot say the same for his family.

During the final six weeks that my husband was away, I kept a daily journal, sometimes writing in it several times a day. I was opening my husband's mail and paying his bills, which caused me to find out much more than I cared to know. Needless to say, I felt angry, upset, betrayed, and stupid, to say the least. I wrote all that I could think of to my husband in that journal. During his graduation from the first leg of Basic Training, he said he learned much about integrity and was a changed man. I really wanted to honor my commitment to God more than to my husband. When my husband returned and read the lengthy journal, he said he never thought those yellow pages would end. We talked and cried and vowed to start over. I told him that all that had happened was behind us, and we would start anew. That idealistic sentiment only lasted the next three months while my husband was away for the second half of Basic Training.

My husband returned from Basic Training on June 30, 1995. Just days before his return, I discovered another lie he had told. I remained calm when I approached him. He dug himself in deeper, and I ran from the house crying hysterically. He followed me, but I sped off in my haste to get away from him. My mind was racing. I needed time to cool off before I said or did something that I would regret. I went to my parents' house and told them I was getting stir crazy waiting for my husband to return. They seemed to buy it and did not question me further. I later returned to our house, but was not interested in anything he had to say. His apologies and, as he coined it, "integrity breakdown" meant nothing to me at that point.

I had taken a Career Development course during my second year at the University of Virginia. During one assignment, we were asked to list three possible occupations. At that time, I wrote adolescent psychologist, mother, and I do not recall my third choice. Even *Even as a teenager, I believed I was called to be a mother.* in college, I felt that I was called to parent. While still in Basic Training, my husband and I talked about starting a family. As a result,

34

I stopped taking birth control pills in April of that year so they would be out of my system by the time he returned home. I also began taking folic acid as well (to protect against congenital spinal defects) to give my child the absolutely best start possible. I did not want to have a baby to improve my marriage; I wanted a baby because it was one of the reasons I got married. I can now admit and accept that my husband and I used each other for different reasons — none of them good. We both wanted what we wanted and reaped the consequences of our decisions.

I got pregnant on Friday, July 6, 1995. I remember the day because my husband and I had not been intimate for quite some time, even after he returned from military training. This is the reason I know precisely when I conceived. In fact, I got pregnant much sooner than I had anticipated. After two weeks, I had the symptoms of my period starting, but that did not happen. My mother asked whether I might be pregnant, and I told her that I did not think so. Nevertheless, I purchased a home pregnancy test and was surprised and elated to see that it was positive. I made an appointment with my doctor to confirm the pregnancy to get a referral to an obstetrician.

Things were going smoothly until August 5, 1995. It is a day I will never forget. It was the first time I felt differently since being pregnant. My mother and I were scheduled to go to Atlantic City, but I called and told her that I felt nauseous. I stayed in the bed for awhile, but felt better after my morning sickness passed. We went on our trip and had a great time; I even won a free lunch from a raffle on the bus. As my appetite was increasing, winning a free lunch was certainly a blessing.

As well as things were going, they began to change rapidly. I was sick ALL the time. I vomited anywhere from four to seven times a day — even in the car. When someone learned that I was pregnant and having some difficulty, I was asked, *"Was this planned?"* My thinking was, even if my pregnancy was not planned, it was certainly nobody's business. I found the question quite insensitive, offensive, intrusive, and judgmental. Anyway, I know that practically every pregnant woman experiences morning sickness, but mine was not relegated to mornings. I would wake me up at all hours of the night. I lost twelve pounds overall and had an internal sonogram to see if the vomiting could be related to me having twins or a complication. I was only pregnant with one fetus. After I lost six pounds in five days, I was hospitalized for two days in August, when I was only six weeks pregnant. The concern was that I needed to be quickly hydrated because women who get as dehydrated as I was could suffer a miscarriage. One of the doctors in the practice told me that the fetus does not get enough oxygen when the mother is dehydrated like I was. I prayed and prayed, and all turned out well. People said how small my abdomen was, but that was because I continually lost weight during the pregnancy. The obstetrician wanted to admit me to the hospital another time, but I declined, in part, because being so dehydrated caused the insertion of the IV to be excruciatingly painful. I was feeling somewhat better. I just put my trust in the Lord that the pregnancy would be fine.

When I was nineteen weeks pregnant, I had my sonogram. I had gained only one pound over my pre-pregnancy weight. I was thrilled with this weight gain because I had regained the twelve pounds I had previously lost plus one! In all, I gained thirty-five pounds during my pregnancy. That is well within the norm, but it generally occurs during forty weeks of pregnancy and not twenty. Once I was able to tolerate food, I ate everything in sight. I was not going to deprive my child, or myself, any longer. I would worry about losing the weight at some later date.

My husband and I had agreed not to look at the sonogram. I really, really wanted a girl because I have a very close relationship with my mother and wanted the same with my child. I was also fairly certain that I would eventually be a single parent and felt raising a daughter alone would be easier than raising a son. In all honesty, I suppose I was also speculating that my husband would be less involved with a daughter. I was thinking, since I want a girl so much, if the baby is a boy, I will have twenty-one weeks to adjust if I find out the sex of the baby. The technician reviewed the results before she invited my husband into the room. I asked her could she see the sex of the baby. She said, *"It is hard to tell, but if I had to make an educated guess, I would say a girl."* The baby moved and she said, *"That looks pretty convincing."* When my husband came into the room, I told him that the technician could not give a definitive answer on the sex of the baby. He never questioned why I had even mentioned this, and I volunteered no additional information. If my child had not died, no one would know that I had looked at the sonogram.

I had gone to many bookstores and even to one library to find books on naming children. I pondered on the names I had selected. Kayla means "laurel" or "crown," and I thought being related to the head might mean she would be intelligent. Symonne means "one who listens" or "one who hears." I thought this name was <u>very</u> important since Kayla's father did not always listen, but I **Names have** **meaning.** also liked my creative spelling of the name. Maybe, some way, somehow, I would be able to override those genes.

Prior to my delivery, I wanted everything to be perfect for my baby. My husband sanded and stained the floor that would be the nursery although he wanted to use the closet in that room for his clothes because he said, *"The baby won't need that much space."* How prophetic that statement soon became. I said I wanted my child to have his or her own space and should they want to be alone or be put in time out, I did not want Daddy to need to interrupt their time. We also needed to paint the nursery. I showed my husband paint samples because the room was pink, and I did not want pink or blue *"I can do all things through Christ which strengtheneth me." ~Phillippians 4:13* because of the sexist connotation. Yellow, I was told, is anxiety producing. So, we agreed on green and purchased the paint. Later, he said, *"Don't you think blue is better?"* I simply replied, *"No."* We settled on a light green for the walls and a darker green for the trim. Days after, when we were sitting at home, he said, *"Don't you think white would be better for the trim?"* Now, what are we supposed to do with a gallon of dark green paint that I paid for? I said, *"No, we agreed on green."* Days after that, I went ahead and painted the trim myself because waiting for him to do it did not seem to be an option. Ironically, that very same day, he came home and volunteered, *"I think white would be better for the trim."* I said, *"It's too late. I painted it green today."* The Lord does work in mysterious ways! My husband looked at the room and said nothing. My mother painted the closet, which had also been pink, because I was about eight months pregnant at the time. She did not want me inhaling any more paint fumes or climbing up on the ladder, as I had done to paint other areas of the room. The room turned out beautifully with the rocking horses that my father had stenciled just below the ceiling. I had never really conceptualized having a theme for my child until I was pregnant. For some unexplained reason, I was only drawn to rocking horses.

Title Unknown
author unknown

God, did you know Kayla was special from inside my womb?
Did You know I would hurt when I left that empty room?
She was taken much too quickly, so early, so small...
But I know she does belong in Your arms after all.

Kayla, I know you've been taken, my baby, but you're
with me all the time
I will always think of you, my darling child, because
you are still mine
I know I can't comfort you or sing you to sleep
But the love I have for you is the one thing you can keep.

Your tiny little tears will be felt each time it rains
But no one can ever help me or take away the pain
Of losing my darling daughter, my joy, my love, my pride
Nothing can hurt more than the pain felt deep inside.

No one can feel the sorrow, no one can understand
How hard it is for me without your tiny hand
I'll always remember your smile and your laugh that was so sweet
And I can picture your little toes and your tiny little feet.

I know I didn't have long with you, but I couldn't have
loved you more

Not from the moment I held you, saw your grandparents walk
through the door
I know you never had a Christmas which I'll regret until I die
You have made one tear that will never leave my eye.

I can't ever pick you up or hold you very tight
And I'll never cuddle you when you are crying out for me at night
But with God at your side there is never anything to fear
Because His love and affection will always be near.

I look up to the Heavens for you and try to get some sleep
Because the baby I once had is no longer mine to keep
Now you are God's little angel who will watch your siblings grow
To be wonderful people and whose love you will always show.

You'll always be a part of me within my heart you'll stay
It's you I'm always thinking of each night and every day
I wish I only had the chance to see you just once more
To tell you, Kayla, I love you and kiss you many times
like I had before.

But now I think of you running around in the Lord's pasture
Skipping and jumping and very full of laughter
With the Lord looking at you full of mercy and love
While you are playing in Heaven far above.

Our time we had together was cut short for reasons why
No one can explain just why you left and made me cry
It's reasons only God can give that can put my mind to rest
For then I'll maybe realize it's true He takes the best.

In every life some rain must fall I've heard that said so often
But when the rain stops, there's a lovely rainbow to tell us
God hasn't forgotten
So take His hand and follow Him wherever He may lead
For He is our Father, He loves us all, and fulfills our every need.

ALMOST TIME

"Nothing else will ever make you as happy or as sad, as proud or as tired, as motherhood." ~Elia Parsons

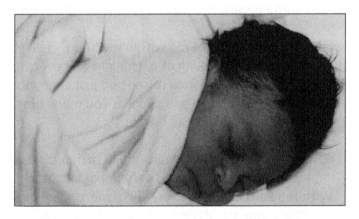

M y parents took my husband and me to dinner on March 29, 1996 – my thirtieth birthday. My father "allowed" me to have a very small sip of wine. My mother and I went shopping the following day and ate at Long John Silver's. My due date was April 3, 1996, but even after all of that walking, there was still no labor. When I got home, I went to sleep, but later woke up and vomited. My husband called my mother to see how she felt because maybe we had eaten something that did not agree with us. She, of course, was fine. Then the chills began. I climbed back into bed and went to sleep.

At 12:23 a.m., March 31, 1996, I woke my husband and told him to let Midnight and Ball T More, our dogs, out. He said, *"They're fine*," and went back to sleep. I woke him up again and said, "*It's time to go*." He got extremely nervous. Considering all the problems that we had in our marriage and the fact that he did next to nothing for me during the entire pregnancy, he was remarkably attentive. I did not focus on the day that he left me alone not only while he went to work, but then to a bachelor party. My memory did not recall the day he commented during one of my vomiting episodes, "*It's not like you had a heart attack.*" He redeemed himself

The easy delivery helped me to focus only on the positives.

during the delivery. He remembered what he had learned during the childbirth classes and was very supportive. My parents also came to the hospital and were in the delivery room with me. I quickly signed for the epidural because the pain was intensifying. The anesthesiologist had to give me two doses because the pain had gotten so severe. After I was given the epidural, I was then in Heaven. Thankfully, I did not need an episiotomy and at 6:53 a.m., Kayla Symonne Anthony was welcomed into the world! I cried and thanked God for my beautiful child. When I first saw Kayla, after my father gave his granddaughter her first kiss, I kissed her and looked her over. Ten fingers and ten toes. I saw what I thought were bruises from the delivery as I was not able to recall all that I had learned during the childbirth classes. The nurse informed me that they were Mongolian spots and Kayla had many. Although others have said I was paranoid, I would verify the Mongolian spots after the nurse verified the numbers on our bands to see that I was being given the child I delivered. Too much was at stake and being paranoid was not a concern of mine. Since then, there have been several accounts of families raising a child for years who was not biologically related to them due to a hospital mix up so my fears were not unfounded. Kayla was born on Palm Sunday. While still in the delivery room, and very early that morning, I called to tell everyone of my blessed news!

When I got into my room, the nurse volunteered that so many babies were born that day, probably because mothers did not want their children born on April Fool's Day. That was true of me! I had many dates on which I did not want Kayla to be born. My due date was April 3, 1996. I preferred that Kayla not to be born on the thirteenth because eventually she would have a birthday on Friday the 13th, and I did not want her to be born on my birthday because I, yes selfishly, wanted to reserve that one thing for myself. I knew I would be sacrificing much as a loving, nurturing parent and wanted that one day for me. I did not want Kayla to be born on April 11 (my parents' anniversary), April 12 (my grandmother's birthday), or April 15 (tax day). Being born on March 31 was totally fine with me. We were discharged the following day. In retrospect, now that Kayla has died, I am grateful that she was not born on my birthday because her birthday has traditionally been a very difficult day for me to handle—even harder than the anniversary of her death. God wanted Kayla to be born on her own special day and granted my request, which means the day is no more emotional for me than it needs to be. Since my birthday comes prior to Kayla's birthday, I can celebrate my birthday guilt-free and then feel whatever emotions are to come two days later on her birthday.

MOTHER-Name		Hospital No.	INFANT-Name			Hospital No.
Anthary, Tonya			Anthony Baby			
Printed Number on Identification Band	Signature, Person Applying Identification Band		Infant's Birth Date		Time	Sex
27471			3/31/96		6534m	Girl
Signature, Person Taking Prints			Color or Race		Weight	Length
			Black		7-6	
MOTHER'S RIGHT INDEX FINGERPRINT		INFANT'S LEFT FOOTPRINT (or palmprint)		INFANT'S RIGHT FOOTPRINT (or palmprint)		

You still touch our hearts
author unknown

in many ways;
you lift our spirits
with a gentle gaze.
Your benevolent eyes
glow with eternal love,
a soothing light
from Heaven above.
Your radiant smile
are emerging sun rays,
piercing the clouds
and brightening our days.
The warmth of your hand
and the sound of your voice
rejuvenates our souls
and makes us rejoice.
You have the gift
of eminent grace;
God blessed you
with an Angel's face.

FORCED TO MAKE AN IMPOSSIBLE AND GRAVE DECISION

"The sky never falls no matter how hard it rains. God's love for you never fails, regardless of your pain." ~Thomas Nelson

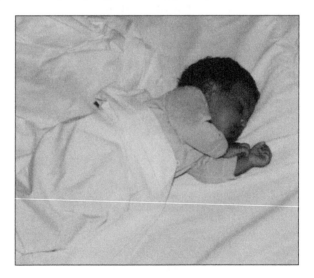

My husband and I decided to go home that Thursday night, one day after the horrific accident, in an effort to get some rest and to pray. We continued to have differing opinions of whether to allow Kayla to remain on life support. We lit a candle and decided, *"Should the flame go out, we will turn off the life support, but should it continue to burn, we will leave it on."* During this time, I reflected on the comforting words of my assistant minister when she said that

Kayla was in a "win-win" situation. She felt that if we removed the life support, Kayla would either return to the child that we knew before the accident, or she would return to our Heavenly *We needed time to be alone to make decisions, hear God, and allow Him to do His work.*

Father. Thinking of the unimaginable situation in those terms helped me greatly as it brought much peace. I remained in a position to make decisions for my child and knew that I would be guided to do what was best for all involved.

I talked to some friends on the telephone as word was getting out about the accident since that first night at Children's Hospital. I had gone through my telephone book and called practically everyone, just as I had done the morning of Kayla's birth, so they could pray for us. Many people called long distance. One friend was trying to cut her Florida trip short so that she could be with us. Another friend followed behind me at some distance whenever I walked the halls in the event I needed anything. Of course, I did not sleep well that night, but it was good to get away and at least pretend that perhaps things were not as bad as they really were.

My mother remained at the hospital. She and I had a three-way call with the babysitter and eventually were successful in convincing her to go see Kayla. I was convinced that she needed time not only to witness the situation, but also to say goodbye. The babysitter did not arrive until around 11:00 p.m., but was able to see her due to the dire circumstances and the fact that she was able to convince the staff she was an out-of-town relative. The babysitter was afraid that people would be angry with her so, understandably, she waited until there was practically no one there. She and my mother visited with Kayla. The babysitter said that it helped her to say goodbye and to see that at least my mother and I did not blame her for my beloved daughter being in such a frightful situation.

When I decided to try to get some rest, I turned off the ringer on the telephone and turned down the answering machine. In a panic, a thought suddenly occurred to me, "What if Kayla should somehow wake up or again go into respiratory or *It has been said, "If we have a problem man can solve, we really don't have a problem."*

cardiac arrest?" I called the hospital and Kayla's nurse answered the telephone. She said that she did not expect anything to happen, but agreed to write down the telephone number of my next door neighbor who would knock on the door should the hospital not be able to reach us. This nurse talked to me for about forty-five minutes that night – until around 11:30 p.m. I asked her whether, in her experience, the death of a child brought couples closer together or tore them farther apart. She said she had seen it go both ways. Miracles happen daily, yet I think I knew even then which category my husband and I would fall into.

When I woke up the morning of Friday, September 6, 1996, I called the couples' therapist my husband and I had been seeing for marital counseling. It was about 4:20 a.m., and I was expecting his answering machine to receive the call. Surprisingly, he answered the telephone. As a therapist, I believed he would anticipate that at that hour, there must be some type of emergency, but he was obviously very annoyed and said to call later. Since he never questioned whether there was any emergency, I never told him that Kayla was dying. Months later, I wrote him a letter. After receiving my letter, he tried to contact me many times without success as I avoided his call when I saw his number on the caller ID. I eventually decided to accept his call and deal with what I anticipated was to come. When he learned about Kayla, he apologized for his behavior. I will admit that I continue to struggle with forgiveness because if I had been suicidal, his apology would have been meaningless to my family members and friends.

After speaking with the therapist early that morning, I called a friend from church, who met us at the hospital the first evening. It was about 6:00 a.m. We talked about her son, who had died during her eighth month of pregnancy. She told me about that experience and how everything was handled. Again, it was comforting to know that I was not alone and that there was someone there who understood, to some degree, how difficult this all was. I say to some degree because all of our children are extra special to us and our relationships with them are unique. Although a mother might know what it is like to lose **her** child, she does not know what it is like for me to lose **my** child and vice versa. My husband and I lost the same child, but even our experiences of that traumatic event are different.

To this day, I thank God that I have no feelings of guilt to deal with as a result of my decision to remove the life support. I have often said that my pregnancy was a modern-day Immaculate Conception because I feel that God gave Kayla to me. Although I do agree with Iyanla Vanzant when she stated, regarding her own deceased daughter, *"Her life was My business and not yours. I didn't give her life, I brought her into life."* She realized her daughter's life did not belong to her yet I frequently saw and continue to see Kayla as "my" child—God's gift to me.

I Found a Penny Today
by C. Mashburn

I found a penny today
Just laying on the ground
But it's not just a penny
This little coin I've found
Found pennies come from Heaven
That's what my Grandpa told me
He said Angels toss them down
Oh how I loved that story
He said when an angel misses you
They toss a penny down
Sometimes just to cheer you up
To make a smile out of a frown
So don't pass by that penny
When you're feeling blue
It may be a penny from Heaven
That an Angel's tossed to you

A LETTER TO MY CHILD

"In the darkest hour, the soul is replenished and given strength to continue and endure." ~Heart Warrior Chosa

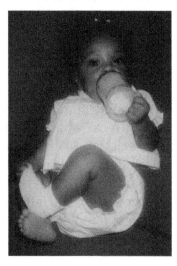

After my early morning conversation with my friend and while my husband was still in the bed sleeping, I decided to write a letter to Kayla. God was prompting me to know that this was going to be the last day of her life. I wanted to thoughtfully consider and then read to her what was on my heart to say while she still had breath remaining in her body. I put many of Kayla's pictures in frames and sat them on the coffee table in the living room. I lit a candle, said a prayer, and began to write. I take absolutely no credit for what came forth because I had all intentions of writing a simple letter. However, the first thing I wrote on the paper was the title of what turned out to be a poem. This made it clear to me that the poem was written before I even sat down to write it. To whom can I give credit? No one, but God.

Fear thou not; for I am with thee: be not dismayed; for I am thy God: I will strengthen thee; yea, I will help thee; yea, I will uphold thee with the right hand of my righteousness.

As I was writing early that morning, the "letter" was getting quite long. I was anxious to get back to the hospital, so I sat down at my computer and typed what was on the paper. Miraculously, more words continued to pour from me with ease. Beyond a shadow of a doubt, I instantly realized I was the transcriber and not the author due to the length of the poem, that fact that it rhymed, and because I was definitely not in a "creative" mood.

My husband came into the room, and I told him I was not ready for him to read what I was writing yet. He respected my wishes and left the room. I wanted Kayla to be the first to hear what was, at that point, supposed to be only for her ears. The entire poem was practically written and typed before we got to the hospital with the exception of a few lines.

> *"Fear thou not; for I am with thee: be not dismayed; for I am thy God: I will strengthen thee; yea, I will help thee; yea, I will uphold thee with the right hand of my righteousness."*
> *~Isaiah 41:10*

A woman my husband and I met in the couples' Bible study of another church was going out of town and stopped by our house that morning around 7:30 a.m. I do not recall what she said, but her presence and hugs were much appreciated. My husband and I got some things together and I carefully chose a dress for Kayla. My husband saw what I was doing and asked, *"What is that for?"* I simply replied, *"Just in case."* He became angry and left the room. I made a few telephone calls, and we were off to the hospital.

FINAL HOURS

"Sometimes God calms the storm – and sometimes He calms us in the midst of the storm." ~Thomas Nelson

The doctors told us that Kayla had failed the test [Brain Death Evaluation] a second time, so we needed to decide when, not if, to turn off the life support. Kayla was born at 6:53 a.m., so I requested that the machines be turned off at 6:53 p.m. My thinking was that she could leave the world at the same time she had entered. The hospital staff agreed to the time I requested, which gave us time to inform others so they could be present if they chose to be.

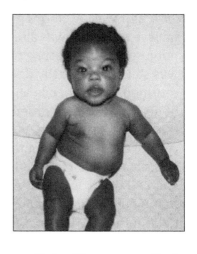

When it was decided that we would turn off the life support, Kayla was moved into a private room instead of remaining in the large open, communal space. That was so wonderful, thoughtful, and appreciated because it gave everyone, including Kayla, some privacy. Having the machines turned off several hours later gave my husband and me a chance to spend individual, uninterrupted, and unobserved time with her. I read the poem to Kayla and made a few changes as I lovingly held her in my arms. Obviously, I wanted my child to be interactive with me, but I

Sometimes God says, "No," and the unthinkable happens.

was willing to accept her as she was at that moment in time and did not want our time together to ever end even if it was in that sterile hospital room.

We all visited with Kayla throughout the day. I now honestly believe within my heart that Kayla was dead long before the life support was officially stopped. I remember it was clear that she was alive initially because of the irregular breaths she was taking and the fact that her pupils dilated at times. However, when I would hold Kayla in the rocking chair, the hospital staff attempted to reposition the tubes so that I could hold her more comfortably without the tubes being twisted. Once, a nurse disconnected one tube to get all the wires untangled. I was previously told that once we decided to turn off the life support, her death would be immediate. Disconnecting the tubes and immediate death was not comprehensible for me with all I was attempting to internalize. Soon after, I was lead to believe that Kayla was already dead because, otherwise, they could not justify disconnecting the tube before the designated time if she was still alive. It really does not matter the actual time that Kayla returned from whence she came because I chose her official time of death which is recorded on her death certificate. I am grateful to the hospital staff who, during that ordeal, afforded me whatever control and involvement they could. During that time, I honestly am not certain what I felt. Perhaps a surreal or out-of-body experience? This certainly could not be my reality. Too many plans for the future that would definitely and unfairly be left to be forever unfulfilled. I was definitely in shock because of the magnitude of what was being "taken" from both of us, but I believe I also felt overwhelming sadness, fear of what the future would – and would not – hold, and peace simultaneously. This was yet another ironic experience of being empty and filled simultaneously. I obviously had a plan, but I willingly submitted to the One that has a Master Plan.

Hours before she died, I read the poem, "Mommie's Bright Sunshine," to Kayla. Of course, I told her that I loved her and would miss her eternally, but I also played some gospel music we used to listen to together. One of my husband's aunts offered to get a tape by Mahalia Jackson that she had in her car so that we could have a variety of music. I was appreciative of the offer, but declined since the tape I played was a tape Kayla and I listened to both at home and in the car. Although it kept repeating over and over and over again, I did not care because I wanted Kayla to die with something familiar to her.

This was all about Kayla.

Just prior to Kayla's death, I was in the family conference room and the telephone rang. A foster parent assigned to another social worker, who happened to have had a son born about six weeks prior to Kayla, called. She asked to speak to that social worker, and I informed her that she had left. She said, *"I heard something happened to the baby."* I said there is nothing wrong with her baby, it was my baby. The foster mother insensitively said that she was glad the other social worker's baby was fine and readily got off the telephone. I was extremely hurt that she did not show any concern for my child or for me, so I mentioned it to the social worker at a later time. She was apologetic of that foster parent's lack of concern and became angry when she learned what happened.

My husband's mother told me many times about how nice Kayla's homegoing was with the music and the number of people around to support us all. It seems as though my husband's family really gained a lot of respect for me throughout that tormenting ordeal. Although I was touched that they were beginning to accept me and my decisions, I remained conflicted as it was such an all-encompassing event to get noticed and to feel valued by my in-laws at a time when it was hard for me to really divert my attention to absorbing any of it.

An hour before Kayla passed, one of the nurses asked me if I wanted to help her get Kayla ready. I jumped at the chance and was shocked, yet relieved, that I was even able to do that. I changed Kayla's diaper, bathed her, and removed some of the tubes taped to her chest and leg. I was able to comb her hair and put on the dress that I had brought "just in case." Kayla's dress was white with pink rose buds and green leaves that I then noticed she had remarkably outgrown. She

People have said they can see the anointing on me.

had so many clothes given to her and purchased that it was rare for her to have worn anything twice. It was not until then that I realized Kayla had outgrown the dress and it was too short. Her socks clashed and my husband said, *"They don't match!"* It was actually a lighter moment because he knew how obsessed I was with having her color coordinated. Kayla had seven pacifiers of various colors so that she would be totally matched from head to toe in whatever outfit she wore. Amazingly, another nurse found some knit booties that had been donated to the hospital by a caring and talented angel. Kayla's outfit was complete. Considering the circumstances, she looked as beautiful as she always did.

Many people were there to surround Kayla and to say goodbye during her final hours. My mother later told me that the nurses had to walk out at one point because they, too, seemed to be overcome with emotion. What a blessing to see the humanity in all while they absolutely remained professional at all times. The Lord can touch anyone during an unanticipated time or in an unexpected place. Members from my family, church, and friends surrounded the bed, and I held Kayla while my husband held us. Everyone was crying so hard. It was incomprehensible that we could be in such a situation. I did not want that evening to come to an end because then I would be forced to face my new and altered reality. Not only would I need to face the future without my child, I would have to leave my precious child in the care of

Even relative strangers where deeply affected by the brief life of a child five months, six days old. She was born to die and impacted more lives after her death.

someone other than myself. This was an unimaginable journey that I did not feel prepared to take. The families were close for that moment in time, but I knew that it most likely could not last. I can only speculate, but I believe my husband must have felt that he wished he had done some things differently and made more of the time he had with his daughter. I had said that I wanted to hold Kayla close to my breast when she died because the one thing that always calmed her was when I nursed her. My father used to say, *"That girl is eating again!"* She and I had both always enjoyed nursing, and it was the one thing only I could provide for her. I think it was all a good plan. The respirator was turned off and Kayla's life here on earth came to an immediate end.

The Anniversary
by Coleman Alldredge

I cannot believe it's the anniversary
That death came and carried you away
Sometimes I feel as if time has stood still
And your death was only yesterday
My heart was replaced with emptiness
Where love for you had been
I did not willingly replace you
Grief showed up and moved right in
Slowly I'm pushing out this grief
Replacing it with memories of you
My love and thoughts are refilling the space
I'll never let this grief replace my love for you
I have never lost my love for you
This grief has only temporally separated us
Grief does strange things to a parent
But never will it replace the love I have for you
Time has a way of bringing healing to a heart
Even though the pain and sorrow may stay
God will always get me through each day
When I reach Heaven He will take all my pain away
Until God brings us together
I want you to always remember
No matter the feelings or things I may say
My child, my love for you is forever

THE AFTERMATH

"A dewdrop acts out the will of God as surely as the thunderstorm. God cares little about size; He cares immensely about service." ~Thomas Nelson

Many people said the babysitter was neglectful because putting an infant in a crib is commonsense. I never had any concerns about her care for Kayla. My response to others has consistently been, "I do not blame the babysitter." If she were neglectful by putting Kayla asleep on the bed with pillows around her, then I have also been neglectful because I had done the same thing many times over. Even to this day, I thank God that the accident did not happen with me or my mother because that would be an additional burden to bear. I believe it was Kayla's time to go and if the accident had not occurred that way, something else would have happened to take her away from us. I believe, regardless, she would have died on September 6, 1996.

The foster parent who worked in the emergency room came to pray over Kayla after her death. Another one of my girlfriends arrived after Kayla's death. She said it stopped raining about ten minutes to seven, and the sun was shining so brightly. Again, the life support was turned off at 6:53 p.m. My girlfriend said she took notice of the time because she knew when we were going to turn off the life support. The weather had changed so drastically so suddenly. This was significant because my friend said she recalled a first grade childhood story in which the rains ceased, and the sun shone when a character died. The story suggested that when this occurs, the Heavens are welcoming the newly deceased person Home. Whether this actually happens is irrelevant because it has brought my mother and me a great deal of comfort thinking that the angels were patiently awaiting their own.

After Kayla died, the wonderful critical care social worker, who joined Kayla in Heaven exactly one year later, was so creative in helping me to get mementos. She helped me to get footprints and fingerprints as well as a lock of Kayla's hair. I decided to cut a lock from the front and one from the back since the textures were different. I thanked the social worker for all of her help and questioned why I had not thought to do those things. The social worker put my mind at ease *Trust in the Lord with all thine heart; and lean not unto thine own understanding. ~Proverbs 3:5* when she simply said, "*How could you know? You've never been in this situation before.*" I immediately thought, "*Thank God that's true!*" Those few words from the social worker helped me to realize that I was not a bad mother for not thinking clearly during that time. Again, it may not all be rational then to have thoughts of being a bad mother as I had done all that was required of a good mother and perhaps even more. I am a perfectionist and much too critical of myself. I recalled the time I was going to a wedding and needed to get Kayla to drink from a bottle. She was not at all interested! I called my mother crying hysterically because I had no idea of what to do. She suggested that I rub the nipple of the bottle to my nipple in order to transfer my scent. It worked as Kayla soon began to accept her alternative source of nourishment. I was continually thanking God for putting people in my life to guide me and think for me during my five months of mothering my child, and especially while in the hospital since I was unable to do much independently. The social worker also suggested to my mother that we put Kayla's last clothes in a plastic bag because it would help to preserve her smell. Although I did that and know the night clothes that she last wore, it really did not work because I was always bathing her! When I have tried to get Kayla's scent, the bag just smells like laundry detergent. That is okay, though, because I am glad she always smelled clean and fresh.

When the machines were no longer breathing for Kayla, people took turns holding her in the rocking chair. After everyone who wanted to hold her did, my husband and I turned the lights out and said goodbye privately to her. Through tears, we kissed her and told her we loved her and would miss her. In all honesty, it was somewhat disgusting that all these body fluids started to be released from her body, but I used her dress that I had carefully chosen, and a blanket to dab quickly so that the fluids did not get over everything. We stayed with Kayla for about two hours after she died and rigor mortis began to set in. After we

The final goodbye was difficult yet peaceful.

were through, I held Kayla up and put her arms around me so that she could give me one last hug. I squeezed her tightly and laid her down on the bed like I did every night. The original nurses had left, so a nurse from another shift had taken over. The social worker got our parking passes validated so that we would not have to pay. My parents, my husband and I went home. I have absolutely no recollection of the ride home. I recall pulling out of the hospital parking lot and then being in my driveway. I do not recall falling asleep, but I have no idea what happened between those two points.

Early the next morning, about 9:05 a.m., I called my church to inform them of Kayla's death and to begin making funeral arrangements. The hospital had been so understanding and gracious to us that my husband and I decided that in lieu of flowers, we would request that donations be made in Kayla's name to the Pediatric Intensive Care Unit of Children's Hospital.

After calling the church, I called a friend in Kentucky because it happened to be her thirtieth birthday. I told her *"Happy Birthday"* and said that if the circumstances had been different, Kayla and I would have sent her a birthday card. She appreciated the call, but I later learned that she convinced the friend that shared the story of the rain ending that I must have been in denial about Kayla's death. I have been in denial about many things in my life, but never the death of my beloved child. Instead of pretending that life was or would be the same, I was attempting to accept my new "normal." Then and now, I live my life as I see fit and try not to worry about anyone else's opinion of me. Many times, I have said, *"What others think of me will not get me in nor keep me out of Heaven."* Most importantly, what God thinks of me is ultimately the only thing that is important and secondly, what I think of myself. Life was already beginning to move on. The flip side to that, of course, is that I wish Kayla was still alive, but that fact is a reality for me every day that I open my eyes.

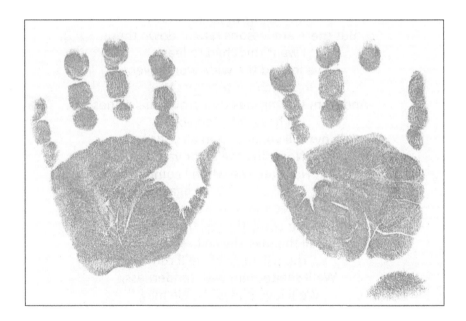

A Child of Mine
by Edgar Guest

I will lend you, for a little time,
A child of mine, He said.
For you to love while he lives,
And mourn for when he's dead.
It may be six or seven years,
Or twenty-two or three.
But will you, till I call him back,
Take care of him for Me?
He'll bring his charms to gladden you,
And should his stay be brief.
You'll have his lovely memories,
As solace for your grief.
I cannot promise he will stay,
Since all from earth return.
But there are lessons taught down there,
I want this child to learn.
I've looked the wide world over,
In search for teachers true.
And from the throngs that crowd life's lanes,
I have selected you.
Now will you give him all your love,
Nor think the labor vain.
Nor hate Me when I come
To take him home again?
I fancied that I heard them say,
'Dear Lord, Thy will be done!'
For all the joys Thy child shall bring,
The risk of grief we'll run.
We'll shelter him with tenderness,
We'll love him while we may,
And for the happiness we've known,
Forever grateful stay.
But should the angels call for him,
Much sooner than we've planned.
We'll brave the bitter grief that comes,
And try to understand.

MAKING THE FINAL
ARRANGEMENTS

"Worry makes mountains out of molehills. God makes mole-hills out of mountains." ~Thomas Nelson

My family had used the same funeral home for years in order to funeralize many of my maternal relatives such as my grandmother, my great-grandmother, my great-great uncle, and others. The funeral home receptionist was initially compassionate and helpful. However, the experience with the funeral director was 180°different. After speaking to her that Sunday morning, the owner was unexpectedly impatient and advised me to call back before 10:00 a.m. with the obituary completed, as she was leaving for church at that time.

I did as I was callously instructed and after reading the obituary to the funeral director over the telephone, she strongly discouraged a separate wake as she did not feel that it was necessary for an infant. The entire time, I was trying to figure out whether she thought it was not necessary because she thought not many people would be present for such a young child, or if it was because it would be too hard on the family. I made every attempt to give her the benefit of the doubt and hoped it was the latter, but something in my gut told me otherwise.

Sometimes those in a position to ease your burdens are really not the ones to show compassion.

Between 2:00 p.m. and 2:30 p.m. that same day, I realized that a paternal great-grandmother's name had been omitted from the obituary. I attempted to contact the funeral home directly, to no avail. In desperation, I called The Washington Post in order to make the Monday deadline. In talking to the newspaper, I had been advised that no fax or telephone call regarding Kayla's obituary had even been received, but the deadline was not until 5:00 p.m. About a half hour later, the funeral director called, extremely infuriated, inquiring as to why the newspaper had been contacted directly. I told her that a significant relative had been omitted. She reminded me that this was why she instructed me to write a draft. I informed the funeral director that there had been a great deal of pressure to meet what amounted to a half-hour deadline. I was thinking, *"My child just died. Why is this person reprimanding me? How has she been able to be successful in her profession for some many years as she needs to attempt to comfort people during a difficult time in their lives?"* In no way did I sense that I was being treated with dignity and respect as anticipated. The funeral director also stated that adding this relative would probably increase the cost by one line. I told her that due to the relationship, this was not a concern. In turn, I became frustrated with her because it seemed as though she did not appreciate me going over her head and taking care of things myself. *"What else was I supposed to do?"*

On Monday, September 9, 1996, Kayla's obituary appeared in The Washington Post as agreed, but her name was spelled incorrectly. When I again contacted the newspaper directly, the representative stated that the funeral director had insisted that Kayla's name was spelled "Cayla." Needless to say, the funeral director disputed this claim. The representative sensitively agreed to run the obituary the following day at no cost which was another blessing because it was my intention, as well as others, to save the obituary.

During the conversation with the newspaper, I inquired, *"What is the emblem that was in Kayla's obituary?"* I had not requested it and had not been informed that it would be there. I was told that some funeral homes have an emblem that typically adds an additional cost of 1.5 to 2 lines. When the funeral director was supposedly concerned about the number of relatives included in

"Nay, in all these things we are more than conquerors through him that loved us."
~Romans 8:37

the obituary, she never mentioned this emblem for which I would be forced to pay. The nerve of some people! I felt that the emblem was free advertisement for the funeral home and wondered why she did not suggest its omission if she was truly trying to save me money. I felt that I was being taken advantage of during my time of need and to this day, refuse to use their church fans advertising their business placed in church pews.

That morning, at about 10:00 a.m., my husband, my parents, and I went to the funeral home to make final arrangements for the service and to select the casket. During the consultation with the funeral home receptionist, she was supportive and considerate of my wishes. She advised us that the cost of embalming would be less than what was typical as less fluid would be needed for an infant. She also suggested the use of a car for the child-sized casket as opposed to a hearse in order to decrease costs. Because the funeral home needed to bring in child-sized caskets before I was willing to make a final selection, my mother and I agreed to return about 2:00 p.m. that afternoon so that we could see which one we would like.

We left the funeral home and went to the cemetery. I wanted Kayla to be buried at this particular cemetery because my maternal grandmother and maternal great-grandmother are buried there as well as several other relatives. My mother's sister went with us because she had agreed to give me her two plots as she and

Even in death, among family.

her husband were moving out of the area and had decided to be buried near their new home. When we arrived at the cemetery, she decided that she felt she needed to keep one plot. Although my husband and I were having problems, I was not thinking of divorcing at that time and wanted to have my family buried together if possible when the time came. I told my aunt that if she was unable to give me both plots, I would simply buy two plots that would accommodate the burial of four people. I called my husband and had him come to the cemetery so that he could help select the burial spot. He knew where my grandmother was buried, but I wanted him to have input of where Kayla would be buried, since she would not be in the section with my grandmother. I tried to the best of my ability to do what was right and include him in making decisions regarding his daughter whenever I could. My mother also decided to purchase two plots so our family has four side-by-side plots. My father, who had previously wanted to be cremated, appeared relieved to learn that he would one day be buried next to his adored granddaughter.

The cemetery consultant was definitely a godsend. He was very kind and patient, even though I had no clear idea of what I wanted for my child. He walked us around to many burial sites and made wonderful suggestions. The consultant suggested a site toward the middle of a section so that there would be less foot traffic over her grave. At no time did I feel the cemetery consultant was attempting to secure a costly sale or rushing me to make a decision as to my daughter's final resting place. Rather, I felt comforted and respected. Due to his graciousness, I sent him a thank you card after Kayla had been buried. The cemetery consultant's compassion was greatly appreciated, calming, and helped me to feel less overwhelmed with all of the immediate and permanent decisions I had to make quickly while not thinking clearly.

Unconsciously, I was constantly singing "Shake the Devil Off" that morning and soon came to understand why. I could not get it out of my mind no matter how hard I tried. Although the devil was not on Kayla, that song was important to me because I wanted the devil to be shaken off those that remained. My mother and I returned to the funeral home and immediately selected the white, metal casket with gold handles and gold angels. The "pretty plush" one looked like a pink Styrofoam ice chest to me and I was so grateful that I had the option of selecting the more elaborate one. My father had insisted that he pay Kayla's funeral expenses as his last gift to her. When we asked whether Kayla had arrived at the funeral home and was downstairs, the funeral home receptionist said she believed so. I wanted to see Kayla so a call was placed downstairs, but the technician was said to be at lunch. I agreed to wait until the next day, the day of the wake, to see my child.

A Mother's Love
by Debra Oliver

A Mother's love
Will never end
Even when for her child
God does send.

Memories of joy
That he has brought
Will be in your heart
And in your thoughts.

Cherish the good times
Erase the bad
It was a special love
That you had.

A certain thing
Or special place
Will remind you of the smile
Upon his face.

Remember his love
With all that you're feeling
And let that love
Promote your healing.

For, a Mother's love
Will never end
You'll just save it up
Till you meet again.

FURTHER UNIMAGINABLE CHALLENGES

"The journey of God starts with one small step. After that, it's one step at a time. He doesn't expect you to run the mile – but He promises to give you strength to go the distance."
~Thomas Nelson

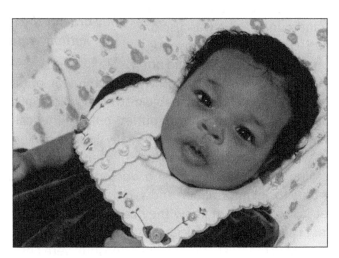

Around 10:00 a.m. on Tuesday, September 10, 1996, I received a call from the funeral home receptionist informing me that there would be a problem with the scheduled viewing time of 2:00 p.m. She needed for me to approve of how Kayla's body had been prepared. Kayla's wake was that evening and had been announced in her obituary in the newspaper. I asked the funeral home receptionist

simply to tell us what time would be good, and she stated that she did not know because the autopsy had not been completed. She went on to say that she did not know when Kayla's body would be available and was uncertain that the wake could proceed that night as scheduled. I became distraught and began thinking, *"I thought her body had arrived yesterday at the funeral home since I was told the only reason I could not see her was because the technician was unavailable."* I asked whether she [Kayla] would be ready for the 7:00 p.m. wake and she nonchalantly said, *"I hope so."* The funeral home receptionist said she would call the medical examiner when he got in at noon. I got his number from her and immediately began making telephone calls myself.

My father is a retired Deputy Chief of Police in Washington, D.C., so I thought he might have some connections. However, he was literally on the verge of a nervous breakdown, so I immediately vetoed that idea. I tried to handle things myself, as is customary, and called my father's police friends and my husband's uncle, who was also on the force. Unfortunately, my husband's uncle was napping and did not

> *God puts people in your life to help you, even if they are not the ones you initially expect.*

appear to want to be disturbed. My husband was outside busily washing his car as an understandable distraction. Now, intellectually, I understand the need to have an outlet, but his physical presence was expected as I needed help emotionally. I called my job's Deputy Director, who previously worked at Children's Hospital, and had others calling the foster parents who worked there. I called another funeral home to get information and asked friends to call the medical examiner just to let them know they cared and were aware of the situation. I called the pediatrician, and she provided needed information and gave me a list of questions to ensure were answered and made calls for me.

When I reached the medical examiner's office, I was told to call the following day. I incredulously stated that this was unacceptable, as Kayla's wake was that evening. The medical examiner hesitantly accepted my telephone call. He unapologetically stated that the funeral home was in error because they had not checked with him about releasing the body. I said, *"I know you've had her body since Saturday,"* and he unceremoniously said, *"We have been backed up since then."* I defiantly replied, *"You may be backed up and performing autopsies is your job, but that is still my child lying over there and I need to be able to move on with this."*

I had been told by the other funeral home to be sure that the death certificate was signed because even if the autopsy was completed, a body could not be released without a signature on that document. The pediatrician called to inform me when the medical examiner had begun the autopsy. Apparently, the appropriate person at the funeral home eventually did what they were supposed to do because Kayla was ready for transport to the funeral home by 1:45 p.m.

The homicide detective later informed us that if I had not been so insistent, Kayla's body most likely would not have been released in time for the wake. With God's help, it all worked out, and the devil was overwhelmingly shaken off!!! That song continually resonated in my mind and spirit for a purpose, but I would be lying if I said I never had any reservations.

"And we know that all things work together for good to them that love God, to them who are called according to his purpose."
~Romans 8:28

Admittedly, I had many doubts as I was relying on others instead of obediently trusting God. The time for the wake was quickly approaching, and I seemed to be running into obstacle after obstacle.

God did NOT let me down!

I had asked the funeral home to provide a draft of the bulletin for Kayla's homegoing service so I could proofread it, which they agreed to do. [Some call it a program, but I prefer to call it a bulletin. A program is given when you go to the theater, graduation, or recital, but when you go to church, you are given a church bulletin.] The funeral home called and said the bulletin had been faxed to them by the contracting agency. I did not have a home fax machine at that time. My husband answered the telephone and said to tell the printer to go ahead with it. I interrupted him and emphatically stated, *"No, I want to see it."* His response was, *"You want to drive all that way?"* The drive was at most twenty minutes, but I ***needed*** to approve of what would happen during my daughter's service. I got up to leave, and he was on my heels. We saw the draft of the bulletin, and I caught five mistakes. As we were leaving, we saw Kayla's body arriving which helped me to breathe a huge sigh of relief. We returned home to get ready for the wake.

I had been going to the same hair dresser for some time. When I called her to see if she could do my hair for my daughter's services, she told me she was "booked." I had put my perm in previously and felt that I needed to put one in as I wanted to look my best for my child. Ironically, while parting my hair, I noticed my very first gray hair. It was unexpected, but not disheartening. I wondered if it had developed overnight due to the stress of the events.

God's Garden
by Melissa Shreve

God looked around His garden
And found an empty place,
He then looked down upon the earth
And saw your tired face.
He put his arms around you
And lifted you to rest.
God's garden must be beautiful
He always takes the best.
He knew that you were suffering
He knew you were in pain.
He knew that you would never
Get well on earth again.
He saw the road was getting rough
And the hills were hard to climb.
So He closed your weary eyelids
And whispered, 'Peace be Thine'.
It broke our hearts to lose you
But you didn't go alone,
For part of us went with you
The day God called you Home.

WAKE AND HOMEGOING SERVICE

"Even a stamp takes a licking before it reaches its destination. Never, never, never give up. God is on your side."
~Thomas Nelson

*F*ollowing this nightmare, the funeral home did not have a second attendee's book readily available for the homegoing service as requested during our initial consultation. My guess is that it was believed there would not be too many people at the wake and homegoing service of a five-month-old child and that we simply wanted to overcompensate. We were told that additional pages would be provided, but instead, friends signed over sections designated for flowers, cards, service, cemetery, and eventually the back of an informational flyer that an usher happened to be carrying.

At some point, a second book was provided, but there were many who were unable to sign anything. A very simple request not being fulfilled means I will never have a record or even know all of those who witnessed Kayla's service and were there to support us as I was much more focused on absorbing other details. I put personal messages in all of my thank you cards – about 450 – so there were many attendees and additional supports that I was unable to contact. I included a picture of Kayla in nearly half of those cards. I sent cards to people who even called or sent cards, in part, because I wanted to include the poem, but I also wanted to acknowledge their compassion and sympathy expressed. Even strangers went out of their way to embrace my family and me.

In the end, Kayla looked beautiful which was my ultimate concern. Getting to that end caused undue stress which required me to be prescribed anti-anxiety medication to ease my continual and profound vomiting and diarrhea. This medication also allowed me to get through the wake and homegoing service. I told my mother that if I died before her and **_no_** other funeral home was available, I would rather she attempt to do the embalming herself than allow that retched place to be used! If the funeral home I used for Kayla makes arrangements for me, I think I am likely to sit up in my casket like Lazarus and awaken from the dead! I know of at least one case in which a friend chose to use another funeral home due to my experience. Since that time, however, the funeral director has retired and has combined with another funeral home. Regardless, I do not want to be anywhere near that place and have even included that in my draft obituary which I have already compiled.

I remember pondering what to wear and decided to wear my pink dress to the wake. For the homegoing service, I was going to wear a green dress that I had never worn before since I had purchased it while I was pregnant. By chance, I had chosen my sorority colors – certainly not a conscious decision. It is ironic to me that when I pledged my sorority, Alpha Kappa Alpha, Sorority, Inc., the line name I was given is "Buried Treasure." My mother pointed out to me that now I also have a buried treasure.

I just went through the motions to say goodbye to Kayla.

I really do not remember getting ready for the wake and surprisingly, I again remember little of even being in the car. On the other hand, I do remember driving home from the homegoing service. Perhaps the finality of it all was just too great a reality for me at the time. I had mistakenly—truly a sincere mistake—taken too much of the anti-anxiety medication and was clearly even less focused than expected. Of course, people attributed my disorientation and fog to the obvious actuality of being a mother whose child just died. The bottle said if there were any mental changes to contact your doctor, but I was certain at the time that I had taken the correct dosage. It was not until the next day when I read the bottle a third time that I realized it said to take one tablet twice daily and not two pills at once. I had reread the bottle twice the first day because I was absolutely aware that my perceptions were a bit off. In the end, I figured that the Lord knew what I needed to make it through that challenging ordeal and mercifully overrode my perception of the actual words. Thank God I did not overdose to the point of needing to be rushed to the hospital because people would have sworn that I had tried to commit suicide. My spiritual beliefs lead me to believe that if I did commit suicide, I would then never see Kayla again in Heaven. I wished more than anything that we were together whether on Earth or in Heaven so perhaps I am passively suicidal.

My husband and I drove to my parents' house, which is when my mother really thought I was losing it although I do not recall her verbalizing it and definitely not within my earshot. She, of course, was not aware of the medication mix up. We drove to the funeral home for the viewing of Kayla's body to ensure we were pleased prior to the wake. She looked very beautiful and peaceful in her white, frilly, satin baptismal outfit. Kayla had on white tights and white satin booties and was holding her colorful rattle. My husband did not want a band around her head because he wanted her pretty hair to show. This was a good decision. Kayla's hair was combed nicely and curly as usual. There had been some hair loss for which Kayla was seen by a dermatologist in August 1996, but that was not noticeable at all. It was quite difficult to be looking down upon my child, but I was very pleased with the outcome. My father was a wreck, but I had nothing to offer to help him. We returned to my parents' house, and my cousin arrived shortly thereafter to take us all to the church for the wake.

Obviously, I entered the church, but only recall walking down the aisle. It does not seem as though there were many people there then, but many soon arrived. A church member had recently been diagnosed with liver cancer, but she had called me and said she would take it easy all day because more than anything, she wanted to be able to attend the wake. She said it did "something" to her to learn Kayla had died. Not long after that, when my mother and I went to visit this person in the hospital, she was unresponsive to us. She did, however, open her eyes momentarily when I said that we were Kayla's mother and grandmother. She died two months later, and I had a vision that she was in Heaven holding Kayla high above her head. Kayla connected to many people in an extraordinary and incomprehensible way during her mere five months on Earth.

For some unknown reason, as others arrived at the wake, my husband and I decided to stand so that we could hug everyone. People are typically sad at a wake, but that night everyone seemed overwhelmingly sad. My husband's grandmother, the one I nearly omitted from the obituary, said she had never been to a wake of a child so young. Certainly, that was part of why people were exceptionally sad, as well as the suddenness of the death of a healthy, vibrant child. All things considered, I was glad to see so many people come out. I talked to many, many people at the wake but do not even remember the majority of them being there. I remember placing a picture of Kayla in the casket as some people had not had a chance to meet her. After leaving the wake exhausted, I fell into a very deep sleep in the car as I rode home. My husband had to wake me up when we pulled into the driveway. Again, I think God allowed me to take the dosage of medication I needed because I was simply trying to survive the events. Once the wake was over, the finality of it all hit me like a ton of bricks. All I could think about was that the next day would be the last time I would physically see my baby, and, therefore, the last time I would be able to touch her. In a warped way, perhaps, I was looking forward to the homegoing service because at least I

God knows the end from the beginning.

could see her again, while at the same time, I was dreading the next day because it would be the last time I would see her in the flesh.

Either that night or early the next morning, I realized that I had not given Kayla her cross and a poem that was given to us in church one Sunday. I got those two things together, as well as the tape so that I could tape them to her envelope with her personally written poem and pictures. When the poem was initially composed, it was going to be something private—between Kayla and me—but I came to understand that they were words others needed to hear. The morning of the homegoing service, I remember practicing the poem many, many times as I paced around my basement so that the flow would be just right. Miraculously, I did not bawl through it as I had done practically every time before. My parents arrived and got ready at my house. It was pouring rain again and my mother said, *"The angels are crying for Kayla."* My husband's family agreed to my request to meet at the house so that we could have family prayer, support one another, and ride in the limousine together. His father and grandmother called and said they would meet us at the church instead. Since we needed to leave soon, my husband told them it was fine to alter the plan and to meet us at the church, but he did not share that information with me. When I asked if his family was on their way to our house, he told me about the call. I was irritated by this news because having all the family together had been my only request to his family, and I wondered why my husband failed to mention the change to me. I was livid. *"Why can't they even grant me this much? Couldn't his family come together and pray together with us now of all times?"* My frustration must have been obvious because it was then that my mother stepped in and attempted to smooth things over. I kept reminding myself, *"I have a gift* [the poem] *I am going to give to my child, and the Lord is going to help me through."*

Again, help can come unexpectedly.

A woman my father had previously worked with on the D.C. police force had retired and now worked for the funeral home I had regrettably decided to use. She was the limousine driver and was one person at that horrid establishment that was very gracious to us. When we arrived at the church, she even helped me with my umbrella. I told her I needed to give Kayla something, and she walked with me to the casket without being asked. I somewhat sheepishly commented that there were so many people in the sanctuary, and she very comfortingly said, *"It's your baby. You do what you need to do."* This caring woman was the one bright spot at that funeral home. When I saw how many people were in the church, I began to get nervous about reading the poem. I did not particularly enjoy public speaking – and much less so at that time – and was unsure of how it would be received. Still, it was something that I knew without reservation I had to do. I am always telling people even now, *"I am just the vehicle by which God's word is able to get out."* He was the One who composed the poem and enabled me to recite it so effortlessly when called upon to do so.

The service was beautiful and, in my opinion, not really very sad. This was in direct contrast to the somberness of the night before. The choir, Voices of Gospel, is normally exceptional, but it seemed it was somewhat difficult for them to sing full force that day. This did not bother me, though, because I understand that the choir members were also moved by Kayla as was everyone else in attendance.

The minister of my church, with whom I had had some philosophical differences in the past, was out of town. The assistant pastor officiated instead. God always works things out! In the pulpit were my assistant minister, my husband's assistant minister, my father's minister, and a woman who I worked with and who I had not realized was a minister until this ordeal. My memory of exact details is a blur. I do not remember very much of anything that people said, but I do recall internalizing what they said was very comforting and appropriate.

My father's minister spoke on 2 Samuel 12:22-23, in which a father rejoices once his son has passed away because, although his son will not return to him, one day he would join his son. My assistant minister spoke of it being a time of reconciliation. Her message was so good that it seemed to touch even those that were not notably religious. This gave me great comfort of how the challenging circumstances could mold together for good. It does say in Romans 8:28, *"And we know that all things work together for good to them that love God, to them who are the called according to his purpose."*

It pleased me and served as confirmation that Kayla's life, although short, was continuing to do God's work and touch people, even in death. Isaiah 11:6 does say *"and a little child shall lead them..."*

I had arranged for one of my husband's aunts to read my poem if I was unable to do so. She agreed, but encouragingly said she believed I would be able to do it. My assistant minister announced it was time for me to read a special poem to Kayla. My husband, who was sitting at the end of the pew, stood up in order for me to get out, but other than that, it did not appear than anyone was moving or even breathing.

"And he said unto me, My grace is sufficient for thee: for my strength is made perfect in weakness. Most gladly therefore will I rather glory in my infirmities, that the power of Christ may rest upon me.
~2 Corinthians 12:9

I had asked that Kayla's coffin be left open during the service, but my assistant minister said that was not customarily how things were done. I had assumed that I would be asked to help to cover Kayla and to close the casket, but I had not specifically verbalized that request to the funeral home. The funeral home, instead, covered Kayla and closed the casket without my assistance. They did not allow me to be as involved in my daughter's homegoing service as the hospital had done during Kayla's last day being hospitalized. I certainly cannot blame the funeral home for not being aware of my desires which I had anticipated would be automatic, but were not spoken. The inevitable had taken place. It was the last time I was to see my daughter's earthly covering. Never again would I see Kayla in the flesh.

When I got up to speak, I kissed Kayla's casket because I had wanted to give her a final kiss. My assistant minister came down from the pulpit to the podium in order to stand by me for support. I walked to the podium and quickly said a silent prayer for God to give me strength and to help me through the reading. I had typed up the poem in large, bold letters so that I would not get lost in the reading. Everyone's eyes were on me, but I did not care. The only ones there at that particular moment were Jesus, Kayla, and me. I felt so honored that God had chosen to speak through me—I was in no way in a creative mood and thus take absolutely no credit for the poem. He allowed me to give such a miraculous gift to my daughter. I had even typed up my introduction because I did not want to leave anything to chance, as I was fully aware that my memory and focus were not at their best. I started my reading by saying,

"During the early morning hours of September 6, while Kayla was still on life support, I was awakened with something on my heart to say to her. What started out as a letter, turned into a poem. I was able to read this to Kayla during my final, private hours with her and see this as a celebration of her life. The title of the poem is

Mommie's Bright Sunshine

On Palm Sunday, March 31, we were blessed with Mommie's
"Punkin," "Wiggle Worm," and "Snooker Doodle" for a little while,
So we should all realize that He chose to trust us with you, His
most precious child.
Mommie tried to do everything right by nursing you, taking care
of herself while pregnant, and not believing the doctor when he
said you might not live
Because through reading the <u>Bible</u>, listening to our gospel, going
to church, and through prayer, you and Mommie know God and
you had so much to give.
Mommie spent so much time selecting and researching
your name,
"Kayla" meaning crown and "Symonne," one who listens, was
perfect because you are the same.
You packed in so much activity and got right with God during your
five months here,
And brought joy, happiness, and peace to those that
hold you dear.
Your light shown through God from above
As He loaned you to us through His perfect love.
I want others to know it is still okay to use your name
Because although you are not here physically, for me you are
still the same.

Mommie, Daddy, Granddad, and Grandma painted your rocking
horse room a light green
Because we did not know if you were a boy or a girl—although
Mommie did peak at the sonogram screen.
You will not grow to be as we imagined you one day as a lady,
But you will always be Mommie's precious, perfect, special baby.
So photogenic Mommie thought you could have a mod-
eling career,
But what Mommie did not know was that you already were doing
your job here.
Who would have thought that while Mommie was taking you on
a plane ride to Busch Gardens, the petting zoo, the aquarium, and
the beach in Tampa, Florida,
You would four months later be at the entrance to God's
Holy corridor.
You went to an African American art museum, took some walks,
went to the park,
Sent cards for special occasions, and hosted a "Mommies and
Babies" gathering in which you sent them home before dark.
When Mommie returned to FLOC from three months' maternity
leave at last,
No one knew that already over half of your life had passed.
I do not believe in corporal punishment because alternatives
work, too,
Which may be why you attended several FLOC functions so that
others could see
Mommie would never spank you.
Mommie knew what school you would attend and bought you
sunglasses and a bathing suit,
And was just starting you on solid foods—cereal, vegetables,
and fruit.
Since you went twice to Durham, North Carolina, once to
Montross, Virginia, and to many friends and restaurants
around the city,
No one need to feel that you missed out on anything or to
have pity.
I had you learning foreign languages even before you could speak,

And so many other plans were made that Mommie thought
would be neat.
Mommie went out and had Daddy, both grandmas, Granddad,
Julie, Diane, Jeanne, Cynthia, Natalie, and Vonda keep you,
Just until it was time for God to always have you.
On July 21 you were baptized with Heather and Eric at your side,
And all those who witnessed know that God will provide.
You had more clothes than your closet or drawers could hold
And had no need that was not met at least ten fold.
Numerous family and friends kept a vigil at Children's Hospital day
and night,
But with God's perfect peace, Mommie can say she had no fright.
Although I wish I could see you as my perfect little girl you were
the morning of September fourth,
Mommie introduced you to two grandmothers and an aunt that
passed years ago and have now taken you forth.
Mommie is comforted to know that you have met those on the
other side,
So there would be no fear on your part once you had arrived.
I kept Vince and Kodak in business by taking pictures of all the
special things you did,
But the special memories in my heart and mind are certainly more
lasting than any photograph ever is.
Mommie kept the bookstores and mail order companies afloat by
buying samples of all in the store,
But God can show you more than Mommie ever could now that
you are at His door.
I was always in Toys R Us getting everything you need,
But now the time has come and Mommie can no longer plead.
Your pets Midnight and Ball T More will miss you poking at them
And Mommie will miss seeing you at the Chuck E. Cheese birthday
party with a grin.
It is ironic to know you were without oxygen at least three times,
But you were Mommie's little soldier and hung on for us all to
have a chance to say goodbye.
I am so grateful that I had the opportunity to give you your last
bath, put on your pretty dress, and comb your hair

Because you had to always be clean and color coordinated, you
always had that flair.
The Maker allowed you to laugh, but earlier to smile your
very first day
So Mommie cannot question or be selfish, but rather send you
on your way.
Mommie has always felt that death was God's ultimate blessing
for a job well done
And know you are in Heaven to welcome Mommie when her
time has come.
You loved being where you were most at peace—outside
And now you are with the Father due to His fantastic journey ride.
Although Mommie is aware that there are many
rough times ahead
She is not ashamed to admit that right now she is doing
fairly well instead.
Because Mommie is comforted to know that once again you are
my precious, perfect one
And you will watch over us all with protection and guidance
until the day when our jobs are done.
You were born and passed both at 6:53
Which shows Mommie her faith was stronger than
she thought it might be.
I keep saying to those with children to please cherish them
because you never, never know,
That in an instant many lives can change and you do not know
where to go.
Mommie blames no one for the tragic accident that hap-
pened that day
Because Mommie knows that God knew what would happen even
before Mommie was conceived and on her way.
But God up above has revealed to me that all is well
Because you will never know the pain and suffering that some
others can tell.
All said how intense, beautiful, strong, and like a doll you were,
The things that were once monumental problems for Mommie are
not important any more.

As we all know, God makes no mistakes
He knew just which grand, happy, blessed, and bright
angel to take.
It is really okay with Mommie that you have gone to a much
better place,
Just know as I do that one day Mommie will have run her last race
and my Kayla Symonne Anthony will be there to greet me with her
bright sunshine face!
May God continue to bless you, those that remain, and always
keep us under His watchful eye
God, Mommie and Daddy and all other family and friends continue to love you and accept that the pain we feel
will ease by and by.

God is good...All the time.

The words flowed so easily from me that even I was surprised. I did not cry, but rather smiled. People later told me that it was obvious that the poem brought me great comfort, and it continues to do so today. I practically know the poem by heart because initially, I read it

Trust God to comfort you and speak through you.

several times a day and for a long time, often recited it in my head. It does not matter to me if I cry through it or smile through it. Sometimes, I recite certain parts that bring me comfort at particular moments during the day. You cannot tell me that God is not good!

I finished reading the poem, returned to my seat, and no one said anything for quite a long period of time. My assistant minister finally broke the silence by saying, "*Wow!*" She then said something to the effect of a person could only do that if they had a special relationship with God. I did not realize just how special at that time, but this experience has undeniably deepened my personal relationship with God. When things like this happen, people often say they can either make you bitter or better. I am not sure if I felt I was better at that moment, but I am confident that I was never bitter. Some people turn away from God, but I turned more toward Him because there certainly was no earthly person who could do anything to help me through that experience. Before Kayla's death, I certainly believed in God, prayed to Him, and could even give examples of how God helped me in various situations, but I never **_trusted_** Him as fully as I am continually learning to, nor did I let Him guide me as I try to do now. I had mistakenly believed that I had more control of my life than was actually the case. Recognizing that you really have very little control over your life can help to ease your burdens because then you do not have to be the one with all the answers.

People told me how moving the service was and that they also did not think that it was sad. I was **_so_** glad to hear that because I knew my daughter had made it into the Kingdom of Heaven so that was in itself a victory. People had gathered to celebrate her spectacular, although short, life. I heard on a television program about a person's light shining brightly although not for an extended period of time, and I think that captures the essence of Kayla's life. What is important is not how long we live, but rather *how* we live. I sincerely believe that Kayla lived her allotted life expectancy which was simply less than any of us could have fathomed. My child did more living and teaching than many people are able to accomplish who live well into old age. For this I am grateful because God moved me to do many things with her and chose me to be the mother of one of His extra special children. Kayla and I "crammed" in many activities as though each day could be her last, but I certainly had no way of knowing her time on earth would be so brief.

The homegoing service was over and as I walked up the aisle, I noticed my therapist, the receptionist from the therapist's office, the hospital social worker, the hospital pediatrician who interviewed us the first day, and Kayla's pediatrician in attendance. It had stopped raining which was great since it was now time to go to the cemetery. My husband and I sat in the limousine in front of the church for a while in order to give people who wanted to follow us to the graveside service a chance to get to their cars. I was able to see more people who had attended since I had only taken notice of few people, while I was in the sanctuary. A longtime family friend, who also happens to be a bereaved parent, came up to the car, held my hand, and said that he wanted to be the first to request a copy of the poem. I said, *"Okay,"* thinking that would be the only person I would give it to. My husband responded to the request by saying to me, "*I hope you are not going to give the poem out because I think it should be something between you and Kayla.*" My opinion is that he was envious because I had asked him to help me find someone to read another poem at the homegoing service, but he chose not to be involved other than to request that one particular song be sung. After turning away from the basketball game after 11:00 p.m. the night I was planning the homegoing service, he said, "*I'll do it.*" I sharply responded, "*If you really want to do a reading, fine, but don't do it to try to please me. It seems that if you really wanted to read something, you would have suggested it hours ago.*" He said that he really did not want to read anything because he would be too nervous.

We left for the cemetery and people tell me that we drove past Children's Hospital. I have little recollection of that, but I know that funeral home drivers often go past a person's residence or where they died. We arrived at Lincoln Memorial Cemetery and drove to the site. I looked back and saw at least 25 cars that had followed us to the cemetery! I am still in awe because of the way it had been raining that morning and because a number of the people who came to support us had never met Kayla. Some came because they had heard of us through others while several had never even met my husband or me. Some said in the cards they had sent to the house that they wanted to connect to me simply as one mother to another. Love and pain are universal emotions.

Following the graveside service, the grounds people got into the grave and scooped out as much of the water and

For those remaining, life goes on.

mud as they could. The cemetery associate had suggested that we request that Kayla be lowered into the ground while we were still there if that was our preference. I said I would like that in order for me to be there to the very end. The grounds people questioned which end of the casket held her head which I was easily able to point out because of the lipstick print left from where I had kissed her casket. The cemetery associate also asked if there were any flowers that I wanted put into Kayla's grave. The one that I do remember having put into the grave with her was the "K" that my father had requested to be designed which was trimmed with pink carnations. We put that in the vault and that was it. We returned to the car to attend the repast at the church.

My parents and some family returned to my house following the repast. It happened to be my maternal uncle's birthday. He and his wife had driven from New York to be with us. We halfheartedly sang "Happy Birthday" which helped us transition our focus from death back to life. He seemed sheepishly surprised and touched. After everyone left, with the exception of my parents, my husband decided that he did not want Children's Hospital to receive money in Kayla's memory. He said that he felt that they should only get the money if they were going to use it to build a new hospital wing. Now, many people supported us and many had already made donations, but there is absolutely no way that enough money was donated to build a wing! I again sharply responded, *"If you had a problem with people making a donation, you needed to say something before the request was put in the newspaper and money had been sent in!"* I never heard any more about that.

It's in the Valleys I Grow
by Jane Eggleston

Sometimes life seems hard to bear,
Full of sorrow, trouble, and woe
It's then I have to remember
That it's in the valleys I grow.
If I always stayed on the mountain top
And never experienced pain,
I would never appreciate God's love
And would be living in vain.
I have so much to learn
And my growth is very slow,
Sometimes I need the mountain tops,
But it's in the valleys I grow.
I do not always understand
Why things happen as they do,
But I am very sure of one thing.
My Lord will see me through.
My little valleys are nothing
When I picture Christ on the cross
He went through the valley of death;
His victory was satan's loss.
Forgive me Lord, for complaining
When I'm feeling so very low.
Just give me a gentle reminder
That it's in the valleys I grow.
Continue to strengthen me, Lord
And use my life each day
To share Your love with others
And help them find their way.
Thank You for valleys, Lord
For this one thing I know
The mountain tops are glorious
But it's in the valleys I grow!

DOING A JOB I WAS CALLED TO DO

"You are never given a wish without also being given the power to make it true. You may have to work for it, however."
~from <u>A Course in Love</u>

I was having many struggles in my marriage, and my husband and I began couples' therapy in November 1995, while I was still pregnant. My mother agreed to pay because she was concerned that my constant negative emotional state might harm my unborn child. We only stopped going as Kayla's due date approached. I really never felt that this therapist was very helpful. This is the same therapist that was annoyed when I called him at 4:20 a.m. I was the one frequently to point out many inconsistencies to him, but I felt it was the best we could do at the time, and my husband was not interested in starting over with someone else.

After Kayla was born, my husband and I continued to have problems. I felt that I needed to look out for myself and my daughter, and thus, made decisions that were in the best interest of both of us. I began, individually, seeing another therapist on May 29, 1996. This is the selfless therapist who I called on the day of Kayla's accident and who attended her homegoing service. I took Kayla with me to most of my sessions, so the therapist got to know her as well. After several sessions, the therapist said she felt I was depressed and in need of medication. She gave me the name of a psychiatrist, and I made an appointment with him. The psychiatrist saw me in August 1996. He prescribed 10 mg of Prozac, the lowest dosage, as I was still nursing Kayla. The psychiatrist felt I was operating on a "reserve" which would eventually "run out." I did not take the medication right away because I wanted to consult with Kayla's pediatrician and my obstetrician first. I had only taken perhaps two tablets before Kayla's accident occurred.

Although there were many appointments with various professionals, I never felt overwhelmed with motherhood. There is no mistaking; however, there was definitely the normal sleep deprivation and having to care for an infant who took over my body and life. Although I was often tired beyond belief, I thoroughly enjoyed being a mother. All my days with Kayla were good days, which has helped to alleviate any guilt I may have had otherwise. She wanted for nothing physically, financially, emotionally, or even spiritually and experienced more in her five months than I experienced well into my teenage years. I remain touched that my father, who rarely gives compliments, once said during dinner at Olive Garden Restaurant, *"You are an excellent mother."* That meant so much to me and still does. I suppose it is the "little" things that make a lasting impression and I am still able to reflect upon that statement. I never fully understood why people would say it was so hard getting out of the house with a baby. I would simply pick up Kayla and her diaper bag and off we would go. It was sometimes difficult going to the grocery store with her because you had to time it when she was not hungry, wet, or tired, but I accomplished that with relative ease. My father had a business trip in Tampa, Florida, in May 1996. Since I was on maternity leave and my mother was also going, I asked if Kayla and I could go. The pediatrician said that the plane ride would not be a problem. I am amazed myself at how I was moved to introduce Kayla to so many things in such a short amount of time, but nothing is impossible with God.

I always thought Kayla was beautiful and had a very peaceful disposition. She was easy going, easily adaptable, and learned to nap in the car. When she was about six weeks old, I saw a commercial on television about getting your baby into modeling. I called and the woman said she needed to be at least six months old. I wrote the number on my October calendar so that I would be sure to call. Unfortunately, I never got that chance as Kayla died one month before that age requirement. However, the photographer from my wedding volunteered to take pictures of Kayla every month until she was six months, again when she would turn one year old, and then annually. I was already in the process of developing her portfolio. I am, of course, glad that I have so many pictures of Kayla. Despite the fact that I thought they were somewhat costly at the time, these pictures are preciously priceless to me now.

I have many special memories of Kayla, mainly of just the two of us. One that I frequently recall is when she was sitting between my legs on the bed, and we were reading her <u>Children's Bible</u>. Kayla was very attentive, turned around to look at me once, and then returned to looking at the pictures and listening to me read. When Kayla was about three months old, we were at my parents' house in the bedroom with my mother. Kayla said what sounded like, *"Hey, Mom."* My mother and I

My infant recognized me as her mother!

laughed about how funny it was that she was already talking, but neither of us believed she made actual words. Then, perhaps one month later, my husband and Kayla were in the living room, and she was in her bouncer seat. I came out of the kitchen and Kayla, who was faced toward the television, turned to me and said, *"Hi, Mom."* I was stunned! My husband had not believed me when I told him about the first incident, but this time he witnessed that Kayla had stopped what she was doing, turned to look directly at me, spoke, and returned to the program that had previously had her attention. I now realize that God was giving me the opportunity to see that Kayla indeed knew who I was, and I am indebted to Him for that in addition to many other things. Kayla also used to twist her ankles which I had never seen an infant do before or since. She had interesting self-soothing habits, but it has helped me to appreciate the individual that she was even at such a tender age.

Maybe once or twice in life we may meet a stranger whose compassion and thoughtfulness leaves an indelible impression upon us that will last forever. Leslie Strauss made such an impression upon me and my family in September 1996.

During the above time my precious five month old grandbaby, Kayla Symonne Anthony, suffered a tragic accident while at the babysitter's. Needless to say, this sweet, alert and vivacious little bundle of joy was the apple of our eye. In a matter of minutes all of our dreams and plans went down the drain. Others may say they understand your feelings but it's like falling off a three story building. One cannot know the true feeling unless they experience it.

Kayla was brought to Children's Hospital and put on life support. Leslie was the social worker assigned to assist my daughter, wife and I, during the lowest point in our lives. Even though we all prayed and hoped, and had support from friends, it was the attending doctors opinion right from the start that there was little hope for our little baby.

Leslie was always there, consoling and assisting us in every professional way. Not once did her compassion, understanding, time, energy or willingness to assist us in every way possible reach the expiration point. My family will always remember and appreciate Leslie's commitment to excellence.

It was truely with heartfelt sadness when we learned of Leslie's premature demise. But we can be assured of one thing, that God only made one Kayla and Leslie, and that they both are at peace with Him.

Leonard A. Maiden

A Head Start on Heaven
by Helen Bush

When those we love have passed away
Our hearts at first are sad,
But here is a thought to comfort us
And a reason, instead, to be glad ~

They just got a head start on Heaven
and beat us there by a little while.
They are already hearing the angels sing
And looking down on us with a smile.

The ones of us left behind
Will miss them here below
But when it's time in God's own plan
It will be our turn to go.

Then we'll meet again in heaven,
And be together for evermore,
They'll be waiting there to welcome us
When we arrive at Heaven's door.

REFLECTIONS

"Seeds of faith are always within us; sometimes it takes a crisis to nourish and encourage their growth." ~Susan Taylor

In the weeks before Kayla's death, I had prayed for peace in my life. I did not see a future for my marriage and was uncertain as to what to do. Ironically, I had a greater sense of peace – although Kayla was gone – than I had when she was alive. I am learning and experiencing firsthand that peace comes from within, regardless of the circumstances, and cannot be granted by another human being. To me, Kayla's death symbolized the end of my mar-

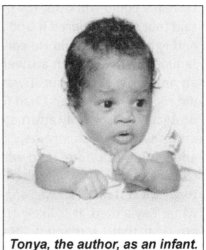

Tonya, the author, as an infant.

riage. My husband and I had no reason to remain connected to one another any longer, as we were never successful as a couple. I am certain that we would have divorced even if Kayla had lived because our problems had nothing to do with what happened with our child. At some point, you get tired of the blanket response to a posed question, *"I have no excuse."* I grew weary of being accused of having an affair when my whereabouts were always known and my friends, both male and female, were always welcome in the house. There were never any secrets on my part or mysterious hang up calls. One of my "friends" thought I must be having an affair simply because I knew a

Our separation was not related to us having our child to die.

married male friend's telephone number by heart. My husband seemed to feel entitled too much, but was not willing to do what was required to have the benefits he desired. He left the home on October 6, 1996 – exactly one month following Kayla's death. When I was trying to decide about the divorce, I wanted it to be in God's timing and not mine. Apparently I had not thoroughly consulted Him about getting married. Others were saying that it seemed to them that God was telling me that I could get divorced, but I was getting conflicting messages and did not feel that the answer was clear to me. I felt that if God could help me to deal with Kayla's death, He certainly could work out my marriage if that was His will. A friend said that she wondered if God needed to come to me with thunder and lightning, or could He come to me quietly. I had set a date of January 1, 1997 for an answer from God. No, He did not give me an answer that day, but it was Friday, February 14, 1997, when I did receive my answer. I had filed for a limited divorce in order to protect my assets. My attorney sent me a letter from my husband's attorney that was extremely inaccurate. I was crying hysterically and could not understand why God was allowing this to happen considering all that I was already dealing with. That is the one time that I am certain that I was angry with God, whereas I had not been when Kayla died. It is likely that I stomped my foot at God, but I am clear that I screamed, *"Haven't I been through enough?! You already have my child!"* Almost immediately, I felt that I had been released from my vows as I literally felt a heavy burden lift from me. My tears began to dry instantly, and I found documents over the course of our two-year marriage that proved my recollection of events. I had no thought of where those documents were if I had looked previously. I never looked back and believe that I was allowed to make the decision that was right for me. In my opinion, we were brought together for a reason – Kayla's birth – but the time had come for us to move on in separate directions.

One morning several months after Kayla's death, I was lying awake in bed and Kayla's name kept sticking with me. I could not get that part of the poem out of my head just like the day when the song "Shake the Devil Off" kept repeating itself. It occurred to me that when people die, it is the belief that they have earned their starry crown which is how the name Kayla is defined. Symonne, meaning one who listens, was also appropriate because God called, and Kayla responded. Proverbs 17:6 says, *"Grandchildren are the crown of the aged."* Kayla's name was perfect for her, and I believe it was selected by God and not me. I imagine that when Kayla's accident occurred, God said, *"Kayla, it's time to come Home,"* and she said, *"Okay, Father."* She rolled over the pillows surrounding her on the bed and by a freak coincidence, a television tray happened to have been placed beside the bed. Kayla's neck was caught in the legs of the tray. She had begun her journey home.

I found it ironic that Kayla died as a result of a lack of oxygen because that was a major concern prior to her birth. I found out I was pregnant on July 28, 1995, and soon became severely dehydrated to the point of losing twelve pounds. I was told that when you are excessively dehydrated, you could miscarry as the baby lacks oxygen. During various points in my pregnancy, Kayla lacked oxygen. When I delivered Kayla, I was given oxygen, but never fully understood why and did not question it because Kayla was healthy. Again, when she died, it was due to a lack of oxygen.

Immediately following Kayla's death, and still on occasion, I feel like I "stand out" particularly to those who know what I have been through. I do not want others to feel sorry for me because I am a mother whose child died. Fortunately or unfortunately, I am not alone because there are many that understand my pain firsthand. When I think of how I am doing now, I acknowledge I am doing fairly well. The way I have learned to cope is not to think about the long distance future. Should I live my life expectancy, which could be as long as forty or fifty more years, I cannot imagine life without Kayla for that long. I literally "take one day at a time" and now know intimately what that means. I once told my assistant minister that I did not feel "empty" inside as some describe, and she said, *"That is because you know Jesus Christ."* I told one of my foster parents that, "*Although Kayla is dead, part of me left with her and part of her remained.*" I told my supervisor, "*Sometimes I do not really miss Kayla because she is so much a part of me, but at other times, I miss her terribly.*" It is so ironic to me that this supervisor and I became such very good friends because she lost her thirty-three-year-old daughter rather suddenly on May 26, 2004. When my now former supervisor's daughter passed, she had five children between the ages of eight years old and five days old. In many ways, Kayla and I are connected more spiritually now than we ever were emotionally. I believe that I am certainly "storing up my treasures in Heaven."

Just prior to Kayla's birth, I had looked into getting life insurance for her. I certainly was not thinking that she would die, but rather was thinking since premiums are set for life, once she got married and had children, she could change the beneficiary and have relatively inexpensive coverage. I thought it would be a good business decision. My husband did not want me to get life insurance on her because, "*It makes death come more quickly,*" he said. I did get him to meet with one company so I knew he was in agreement with getting the life insurance. I decided to go with the original company because of the cost and because my husband was not willing to discuss it further. I put the annual premiums on my credit card so I would not have to think about it every year. Sadly, Kayla died merely three weeks after I was granted the insurance. Although the policy was solely in my name, my husband felt that he was entitled to half the money, since he thought I paid the premiums out of the joint checking account. I proved otherwise, but I was blinded by my grief following Kayla's death and listed my husband's name as the father on the claim form so he did receive half of the money. When I called the insurance company, they said that was the way things were done. Never would I have thought we would be fighting about money so soon after Kayla died. I did not think that he deserved the money not only because he paid no premiums, but he only purchased one pack of diapers for Kayla after being forced to do that. My husband later admitted he did not use the money for anything respectable, but refused to share any of the details with me. I chose to have my kitchen remodeled and see it as a gift from my beloved child.

A few months after Kayla died, I started looking into having a marker made for her grave. It bothered me that her grave was unmarked, and I wanted others to know her name and how much she was and is loved. I invited my husband to the cemetery and met with the cemetery associate. Although I liked what they had available, it was completely out of my price range. My husband selected the second most expensive stone so I got the measurements and explored other possibilities. I decided to use another granite company since the marker was about one third less the cost. Although still expensive, I was willing to pay for it since I felt it was the last gift I could give to my child. When I was asked which flower I wanted engraved, I chose dogwood because it represents Christianity. I had the rocking horse that was stenciled around her room engraved on the marker and requested that it be placed on her birthday. Of course, my husband never offered any money to help pay for the marker, despite his wanting the top of the line and had half of the insurance money coming. When I asked about it and said, *"It isn't like I'm happy that Kayla died because now I have some money,"* he insensitively said, *"Isn't that what you're saying?"* I was forced to give the receipts of all the homegoing service expenses and the marker to my attorney because we were going to court regarding the divorce. Regardless of the physical evidence, my husband still called all the merchants to verify the charges before he would reimburse me for any of the expenses. Since I did not have a receipt for a $75.00 expense, he refused to give me an additional $37.50 which I, of course, did not argue about. His actions simply helped to show me more clearly the type of person he was and left me with no doubt about proceeding with the divorce. About two months after my husband received the insurance money, he reluctantly sent me half of the money for the expenses. When I asked him why it took so long, he responded with his usual statement, *"I have no excuse."* My husband was mad at me because he did not want a divorce and because *"You are the one that got a third party [attorney] involved."* My husband had wanted us to reconcile. He sent me a Valentine's Day card and a Mother's Day card and present. This is interesting since he did not do those things when

One final gift to my precious daughter.

we were together or while Kayla was alive. My husband usually started an argument around the holidays, although he knew how important they were to me. Although I felt I had no choice regarding getting divorced and have no regrets about that decision, I continued to pray and wait until God gave me the answer that He was releasing me from my vows before I proceeded. I felt like I had hit the "bottom," and it was nearly as painful as Kayla's death because I was angry with the only One who could help me. I was not angry with God that He took Kayla Home, but I was angry that He was allowing my husband to continue to mistreat me despite all that I was going through. Without a doubt, Kayla's death was the most difficult thing that I have ever experienced in my life, but I was still trying to come to terms with that loss and did not have the same degree of support with the divorce as I did with the death of my daughter.

I admit there was a time that I was obsessed with Kayla and perhaps "*so Heavenly bound and of no earthly good.*" My therapist felt that I needed to get angry with God about Kayla's death in order to heal. Interestingly, a friend from my church who came to the hospital the night Kayla died said, "*Some people will tell you that you will be angry with God, but that is not necessarily true.*" The assistant pastor reminded me that I did not need to be angry with

God in order to heal, but she felt that perhaps I was angry with God and displaced it onto my husband. My therapist had said that my anger at my husband was not proportionate to the problems we had, but I was angry with my husband long before Kayla's death. Several people feel that I had to have been or "should" have been angry at God, but all told, I do not agree that I was ever angry with God regarding Kayla's death. Now, I have questioned why I could not learn what I needed to learn some other way and still have my child, but that was not God's will. I can confidently say that I was angry at God during the period that was soon to follow so I am in no way attempting to circumvent my feelings.

Some say that the stages of grief as outlined by Elizabeth Kuebler Ross are outdated. There truly is no "right" way to grieve as the process is intensely personal. The stages as outlined are:

(1) Denial and Isolation – "No, not me!"

I did not want to believe my child was going to die. I felt alone, although there were many, many people supporting me because there was absolutely nothing they could really do to help me. I was the only mother of my dear Kayla. As I was reading to Kayla from her Children's Bible that first night at Children's Hospital, everything I read spoke of God's miracles: making a blind man see, the woman who touched the hem of His garment was healed of the issue of blood, turning water into wine, and making the lame to walk. I got right in Kayla's right ear and said, "*I know you can come back to Mommie.*" At that moment, I was in denial of the inevitable.

(2) Anger – "Why me?"

As I stated, I do not think that I experienced anger at God in relation to Kayla's death, but at my husband, most *DEFINITELY*! A bishop in my church reminded me prior to my even filing for divorce that I needed to forgive my husband as the Lord commands. I told him, "*I'm not on the same level as Jesus,*" since I did not see myself forgiving my husband at that time.

> *Forgiveness is releasing the person who hurt you so God can change them. The true benefit is that forgiveness frees the forgiver. It may not be instantaneous.*

The more challenges I have experienced in my life, the easier it has been to forgive my husband. I think I was really angry at myself for not being able to protect Kayla, for not being "connected" enough to her that I could have foreseen this incident coming and somehow prevented it from happening, and for not being a stay-at-home mother because, perhaps then, I would have watched her more carefully. As I said before, I had also put her on the bed surrounded by pillows. In the end, I believe that Kayla had lived the life that was allotted her. Even if she was not hurt on September 4, 1996, I think she would have died September 6, 1996. Maybe the circumstances would have been different, but Psalm 39:4 says, *"LORD, make me to know mine end, and the measure of my days, what it is: that I may know how frail I am."* I saw the parallels and thought Kayla was meant to die on that Friday. Jesus was crucified on Friday and resurrected on Sunday. Kayla was born on Sunday and died on Friday. My husband and I were married on Sunday, September 4, 1994, exactly two years to the day prior to Kayla's accident, and Kayla died on Friday, September 6, 1996. I thought this might somehow be "coincidental."

(3) Bargaining – "Yes me, but at least..."

I did consider bargaining with God as would anyone in such a desperate situation. I initially thought that if God restored Kayla to the child that I had dropped off at the babysitter's home that Wednesday morning, I would try harder to make my marriage work. Quickly, God reminded me that He does not make bargains because it does not control the outcome that He alone determines or predestined. The good we are trying to bargain for is already precious in the mind of God. I came to realize that it would not be fair to bargain because I knew that I had tried as hard as I possibly could in my marriage. I was being the best wife and Christian that I knew how to be, so there was no bargain I could make. I did not want to be bound by God in a marriage that was not good for anyone involved, even if Kayla had been restored because I wanted the absolute best for her. I came to understand that the best thing for my child would be for her to return to her Heavenly Father.

(4) Depression – "Oh no, not me!"

I definitely experienced depression after Kayla's death and still do because of a variety of influences. From January 2004 through June 2005, I was taking an antidepressant. Usually, when I cry really hard, I feel better, and then, I am able to move on. The most horrible day I experienced was her first birthday after she passed. It was even more difficult than the day she died or even the day she was buried. Palm Sundays were initially hard, too, since she was born on that day. In addition, February 12, 1997 was incredibly challenging because Kayla had lived for five months, six days and on that day, she had been dead for five months, six days. As you can imagine, the first Mother's Day was difficult because you question your title if your child has left you, but I am grateful to those who continued to view me as a mother on that date although I was not actively parenting. One person questioned what I was doing for my mother on Mother's Day and was shocked to learn that I anticipated it would be a hard day for me. It seemed as though this person "forgot" that I was also a mother and judged me as being selfish. July 21, 1997 was difficult as that was the day Kayla was baptized and thus began deepening her relationship with God. Other more obvious holidays and anniversaries have been difficult, too, but as my former supervisor and now friend says, *"The longest day has an end."*

(5) Acceptance – "So it is."

It took me a long time to internalize this one. I believe I have accepted Kayla's death because there is little else can I do. Still, there are days that remain very challenging. I cope by keeping Kayla's memory alive by adding relevant poems and stories to her photo album, talking about her, and sharing her with others.

Clinical psychologist, Therese Rando, PhD, has identified the process of mourning and says that people in mourning are to:

(1) Recognize the loss
(2) React to the separation
(3) Recollect and re-experience the deceased and the relationship
(4) Relinquish old attachments to the deceased and the old assumptive world

(5) Readjust to and move adaptively into the new world without forgetting the old
(6) Reinvest

I have done a great deal in honor and memory of my daughter as I have continued to grow and move through this journey.

The opinions of both of these professionals seem to have their value in my life because for a brief moment, I did say, *"Why me?"* I felt as if I was trying to live a life pleasing to God. I went to church, paid my tithes, and tried to be a good steward over my blessings, but God took the one thing that meant the most to me—Kayla. I would often ask myself, *"Why were we the ones chosen?"*

I continually try to incorporate into my life the understanding that God relieves us of our compulsions as soon as we admit that we are powerless over them.

Others have pointed out how God gave His only Son to the world, and how Mary was there to return Jesus to Heaven. Kayla was chosen for a purpose larger than I can ever imagine. Maybe when I get to Heaven more will be revealed to me, but the reality is that not a whole lot will matter then. When I do question God, I know that He is resilient, sovereign, and can take it. Miraculously, He continues to love and forgive me despite my many shortcomings. I try to be grateful for my good moods and to have grace when I am having a bad day. God frequently speaks to me through my children and apparently felt that I was able to help others, as I work through my ordeal. What I have come to realize is that I simply work to do what is right because it is right and not in order to barter with God for additional blessings. I have also been reminded of a quote by Arthur Ashe in which he said, *"I never feel 'Why me?' If I ask 'Why me?' about my troubles, I would have to ask 'Why me?' about my blessings."* Through my trials and tribulations, I have had to learn not to maximize them while minimizing my blessings. I believe God wants us to pray during our struggles and manage them appropriately while being thankful for our many blessings. A church hymn that truly has more meaning for me now and which I love is "Blessed Assurance." All that has happened to me is my story of which the hymn speaks. Another song, *"Testimony,"* states, "As I look back over my life and I think things over, I can truly say that I've been blessed. I have a testimony." Yes, I do have a testimony as a result of Kayla's death, but God helps me to deal with that loss daily. For that, I am truly blessed. I have no control over my experiences, but I do have control over how I respond to those experiences. In other words, in life you must learn how to appreciate the roses in spite of the thorns.

Martin Luther once said, *"God creates out of nothing. Therefore, until a man is nothing, God can make nothing out of him."* We find in 2 Corinthians 12:9, *"And He said unto me, My grace is sufficient for thee: for My strength is made perfect in weakness. Most gladly therefore will I rather glory in my infirmities, that the power of Christ may rest upon me."* When Kayla was hurt, the pit of despair was deeper than I could have ever imagined. I was nothing then. What came out of that was a deeper relationship with God and a greater appreciation of His love for me. I am one who always wanted to be in control, but all control was stripped of me when I first learned of Kayla's accident. It is when we admit that we do not know how to run our lives that peace returns. During that time, I had no where on earth to turn, so I had to step aside and turn to my Heavenly Father. We can think the universe has conspired against us, when the truth of the matter is that the universe has paid us very little attention. God, however, knows all about the universe and is still able to assist us if we are willing to allow Him. We cannot do what belongs to God alone to do. Our job is simply to move aside. Life is often only as hard or painful as we, in our self centeredness, make it.

Death, like birth, is a natural process. It is not a mistake or an outrage. Death is a part of the life cycle and is merely the last stage of living. By finishing the process that began at birth, a person's death makes his or her life whole or complete. The person who is dead has no problems. We, who are left, are the ones with the problem which is our sense of loss. Acceptance of death, like acceptance of our past, is the way of the wise. It says in Revelation 14:3, *"And I heard the voice from heaven saying unto me, Write, blessed are the dead which die in the Lord from henceforth. Yea, saith the Spirit that they may rest from their labors and their works do follow them."* Each of us has a finite amount of time on earth, but it is enough time to do the work that only we can do—the work we were sent here to do. Kayla completed her life cycle in merely five months, so obviously her work was done. Our divine potential is meaningless if we are unaware of it. As our awareness of God's presence in our life expands, we will feel as outlined in Philippians 4:7, "*And the peace of God, which passeth all understanding, shall keep your hearts and minds through Christ Jesus*" regardless what unfolds. Life is a journey back to God from whence we came, and our relationships are the roads we travel. I am grateful that I had the opportunity to have a relationship with Kayla and now to know that I have her as a guardian angel.

Playland in Paradise
by Rebecca Anne Obregon

Where do small children soar on winged rocking horses,
and play hopscotch from cloud to cloud?
Where do sweet babies sleep in great-great-grandfather's arms,
and never once make a tearful sound?
Where do adventurous toddlers explore without ever a fall,
without ever a forbidding, "No, No",
Where nothing can hurt and nothing can break,
and nothing's too high or "just for show."
Where picture-filled storybooks stand row upon row,
with no shelves to straighten or dust,
And thousands of aunties and uncles and grandmas read
endlessly,
never impatient or rushed.
Where there's never new teeth, nor ones to be pulled,
no sick tummies, scrapped elbows, or knees,
No big scary dogs to growl or to bite,
and no stings from buzzing bumble bees.
No nap-time, no spankings, and no lima beans,
no "boo boos", no "uh ohs," no tears,
Just tiny faces wreathed in smiles, high pitched squeals and
happy giggles,
and unbound excitement as their favorite time nears.
Storyteller's at hand, and as the Storyteller stands,
amidst all of the laughter and joy,
Little feet scamper to feel His touch
as He embraces each young girl and boy.
After kissing each tiny saint, He sits down among them,
placing a child upon each knee,
And, softly, the Storyteller begins His story with the precious words
"Let the little children come unto Me."

In loving memory of all children, born and unborn, who have made only short visits here before being called Home to "play." Dedicated to families who have their own "little saints" in Paradise's Playland. Talk to them, they hear you, pray for you, and await your reunion.

SUGGESTIONS

"The greater the adversity, the more profound the wealth."
~Michael Norwood

My life has changed in ways I could not have imagined. In some ways, I think that I am a better person because I have been able to survive such an unimaginable fate. I see my experiences as a catalyst to developing an even deeper relationship with and faith in God. I am learning that what is hurtful can be helpful if we make the conscious decision to grow in wisdom, compassion, and love. Unfortunately, I have lost some "friends," both mothers and non-mothers, throughout this never-ending tribulation, and I understand more fully that nothing can be taken for granted. Some "friends" wanted to come back into my life once I had another child, as if I was now "less damaged goods." It is certainly not a matter of me not believing in forgiveness and striving to grant it, but I do not feel the need to put myself in yet another situation to be hurt again by those who said that they cared about me, yet were not able to bear my darkest hour. I was bluntly told by one such person that it was too hard for her. My feeling was that if she multiplied her pain by 1000, she would only begin to conceptualize the pain I feel. Furthermore, it was not about her or me for that matter, it was about my child. I can forgive people in my spirit for such self-centeredness, but I realize that I no longer need to be "buddies" with everyone. I can wish them well and pray for them from afar. In my opinion, the people who could not put their needs aside to help me when I needed them most need not attempt to share in the joyful times either. The future is open, so I should not be needlessly narrow. Rather, I cast my net more broadly, availing myself to the resources of God, which I realize may be in people that I have yet to encounter.

I was one of eight women pregnant around the same time, which is why I hosted a "Mommies and Babies" gathering at my home so that we could support one another and to show off our blessings. After Kayla died, some of those same women were uncomfortable around me, as if Kayla's death was somehow contagious. Others just did not know what to say and should have remained silent. I was told that I was young and could have another child, which I found demeaning and insensitive. If I had been able to have one hundred children, Kayla could not be replaced. I explained to one person that if my husband had died, she would not suggest that I simply marry again. Someone told me that if Kayla was older when she died, it would be harder because I would have been more attached as though I was somehow "less attached" because she was an infant. I found such statements infuriating. When a young child dies, we grieve more for the future we envisioned that will never be probably more than the past we have embedded in our memories. I asked God why Kayla could not live to see Christmas or her first birthday knowing full well that there would not be an acceptable time for my child to die. When would I have selected a "better" time? My advice is that people do not need to search for the "right" thing to say. When people told me they did not know what to say, I would exclaim, *"That's okay because I don't know what I need to hear."* My mother said that she and my father were talking not long after Kayla died and said that they did not know what to do for me. I reiterated, *"There is nothing you can do, but that's okay because God is taking care of it all."* My suggestion is simply to say to those that are hurting, *"I'm sorry,"* perhaps offer a prayer, and maybe give a hug. People stopping by for short visits or calling briefly was more helpful than any ridiculous monologue which resulted in increased anguish. I was not in a position to "entertain" others or attempt to ease their sorrow. I do not remember most of the things people said to me because I was thinking about Kayla instead of concentrating on their platitudes. Even today, after many years and softened sorrow, I have a great deal of difficulty with my short-term memory, which I believe is a direct result of my loss of Kayla as it occurred so immediately. So, in reality, the less said the better. Showing me that they cared was much more effective and memorable than some flowery words which could in no way numb the pain.

As I have talked to people months or even years after Kayla's death, some have told me why they could not attend the services, but few excuses seem reasonable to me. One person did not attend the service and later stated that in reality, she could have attended as an "important" meeting was canceled. Others cannot understand why I do not recall them being present. I expected people to understand that my focus was on somehow getting through the service and absorbing the final

Sometimes, the less you reveal, the better.

details of my child's life and death rather than tallying who walked through the church doors. While I appreciated the people who were kind enough to attend the services, Kayla was my total focus. Under the circumstances, in my opinion, it is best not to be offended if your presence goes unnoticed. Although I am eternally grateful to all who were there and assisted in many ways, my attention span was very poor and my memory of many events continues to be affected even today. Things have greatly improved, but I now rely on notes and lists much more than I ever have because things leave my consciousness very quickly. Perhaps this was a coping mechanism that allowed me to manage as well as I did.

To ensure my body had healed properly, I had to have the normal, six-month gynecological, post-partum examination. Kayla had died only the month before. The office very graciously sent me a fruit basket following Kayla's death and placed the bulletin in my file. My doctor, whose birthday happened to be the day of Kayla's death, took time to ask me how I was and spent extra time with me. However, I had to return in October 1996 because I was bleeding and could not fathom why. My preferred doctor was unavailable so I saw the doctor who had said I was threatening a miscarriage while I was pregnant with Kayla. Although he had been the one to deliver her, during the visit he never said he was sorry to hear about Kayla's death nor did he ask how I was doing. Nearly one year later, I returned to the office because I was continuing to produce breast milk. This same doctor, who was one out of four in the practice, seemed to always be the one available. He looked in my chart and said, "*I guess you are still trying to get over this.*" My response was, "*No, I will never get over the death of my daughter. I must simply incorporate this loss into my life.*" In my opinion, this doctor lacked any indication of a good bedside manner. It would have simply been better for him to say, "*I'm sorry.*"

When people said, "*God knows best*" or "*It is God's will,*" I did not want to hear that when my child was near death. At that moment, I was vacillating whether God was making His first mistake and why He would not grant my desire to restore my child fully. I had accepted these statements in other areas of my life, but the loss of Kayla was too overwhelming to think that this is how things were "supposed" to be. Over time, I have been able to accept these statements as an attempt to provide *I needed time to process and accept the sudden reality of my situation.* some semblance of comfort to myself. Still, I continue to believe that it would have been better for me to come to this realization in my own time, as opposed to having others try to move me along in the process at their pace. The majority of people readily willing to share their "wisdom" are those whose lives have gone along rather smoothly and predictably, and thus, have very little insight into what I was experiencing. How could they begin to contemplate what I was going through? They could not. I have often told people that they should be grateful for not knowing what it is like. I do not tell other bereaved parents I "know" what they are going through as every child means something totally different to every parent. Grief is universal, but the way we grieve is individual. People repeatedly attempted to be reassuring by telling me, *"You will be blessed."* Of course, the Bible says in Matthew 5:4, *"Blessed are they that mourn for they shall be comforted,"* but at the time, my only thought was, *"Why did my child need to die in order for me to be blessed?"* As a Christian, I know we are blessed daily without the need of tragedy, but during Kayla's hospitalization, the only blessing I wanted was for my child to be whole in mind, body, and spirit again. Of course, as I have reflected further and have had more revealed to me, I can see God is using my experience for His glory. In those initial hours and days, however, that was not my focus, as I was literally in a state of shock.

Overall, my suggestion is for people to simply be cautious of the comments they make to another person because it can be a seed planted into their spirit that may grow into something fruitful, but not how it was intended. I still recall the searing pain of some comments that were meant to be "helpful." If you see a person looking sad or making reference to some difficulty, refrain from sayings like, *"It can't be that bad,"* because it very well may be worse than you can ever know or imagine. A perfect example is when I was leaving the post office one day when a guy made this comment to me. I responded, *"I have a daughter that died so it is."* When I went to get my hair done, the stylist made a similar comment, referring to another stylist who happened to have also lost a child. She was surprised to learn that I also shared a similar history. The reality is that no one ever really knows what another person is going through. It very well could be that bad to the person going through it. "Tomorrow" is not promised to any of us, so we really need to cherish our loved ones today as it could be our last day or theirs.

When I am around new people, I sometimes feel uncomfortable because I never really know what to say when questioned about how many children I have. Usually, I say I have two children and give their ages, although in the last few years, I often volunteer that I technically have three children. When I do not include Kayla in the count, I feel like I am betraying her or hiding the fact that she did indeed exist and continues to be very important to me.

The Grave No One Tended
by Cheryl L. Costello Forshey

The day was lovely as I strolled along
peering at stones on the way,
And that's when I saw it, that pitiful cross
that looked splintered and faded away.
With flowers in hand to tend Father's grave,
I knew I must hurry along.
But I couldn't help but linger while
at that cross that just didn't belong.
The date on the front confirmed my suspicions
of what already I knew.
A child lay beneath that horrible cross
and its faded color of blue.
What selfish parents they must have been
to bury their child all alone,
Without flowers or candles to light the night
and not even a simple headstone.
I looked even closer at that awful cross
that was nearly splintered away.
And there on the back, I read the words
that changed me forever that day.
"This cross isn't grand, but it was carved by my hands
so you'll know, son, how much I care.
It's the color of blue to remind me of you
and how painful it is I'm not there.
That it's you who is gone and it's me living on
while your young life has come to an end.
And I'm left alone, never again with a home
and a grave that's too painful to tend."
Tears stung my eyes as I looked all around
at the monuments that ragged cross put to shame.
And I shared with those parents their horrible loss
that brought them such terrible pain.
And all the tombstones, some even taller than me
suddenly seemed small in a way,
Next to that little handmade cross, carved with such love
and the flowers I planted that day.

113

WHAT MAKES ME FEEL SAD

"We do not get over grief. But over time, we do learn to live with the loss. We learn to live a different life...with our loss."
~Kenneth J. Doka

When I think about the things that I wanted to expose Kayla to and how I wanted to raise her, I experience my greatest sense of loss. Regarding discipline, I had no intention of spanking her because I make every attempt to refrain from corporal punishment. In my many years as a child welfare social worker who interacts with abused and neglected children, I think  spanking children teaches them to solve their problems by hitting, and I also believe it teaches them to be deceitful because they find ways not to get caught misbehaving. Ultimately, in my opinion, children focus on the pain that is inflicted and not on the lesson to be taught. In other words, spankings teach children that others need to be around to correct their behavior instead of them gaining internal controls. I had already started incorporating discipline into my interactions with Kayla, which some did not agree with. As stated, I nursed her. She would sometimes "play with her food" and fall off my breast. I would tell Kayla, "One more time and that's it." When she would fall off and look up at me, I would say, "Okay, you're done." Believe it or not, the next time we would nurse, she generally did not play around, but rather completed her meal. I came to learn the difference between when Kayla stopped nursing and when she was playing.

I had brought some foreign language tapes that have nursery rhymes in six languages. Kayla and I used to listen to them in the car. Although I had absolutely no idea what the people were saying, I wanted Kayla to get the flow of the different languages. Over time, when she learned the nursery rhymes in English, I thought she would have an easier time understanding the various languages. I tried to expose Kayla to everything that I could and obviously wish that I had the opportunity to continue. My plans went so far beyond being a mother of an infant. I feel eternally blessed and grateful, though, that I am able to do these things and more with my two surviving children.

I take motherhood very seriously and probably to an extreme in some cases. I even made all of my children's baby food. I have a juicer and would put the food in there first. I would then put the pulp and juice in a pan on low heat with purified water. Once the food was the right consistency, I would freeze individual servings. Kayla ate carrots, peaches, apples, peas, sweet potatoes, and I had prepared green beans, but she never had the chance to try those.

I did many things myself because although time was limited, money was even more restricted. I am far from being independently wealthy, but I remain rich in the blessings bestowed upon me. I usually brought all of my children's needed items from consignment stores or with Toys R Us gift cards. Many necessities were given to me by relatives and friends. A cousin gave me an infant car seat which my mother kept in her car since I had an infant/toddler seat in mine. That cousin and another one gave me clothes for Kayla up to size 4T, so I was prepared for years to come. All of the clothes, separated by size, were packed up and stored in my subbasement. My children may not have always had "new," but they have had decent and "new to them" clothes. They have never been in need of anything—which is clearly very different from wanting something. I had opened a savings account for Kayla after a church member gave me money for her "college fund." Thanks to my mother, Kayla had a mutual fund to go toward her college education to which I was able to contribute as well, which was another reason I made every effort to conserve wherever and whenever I was able. All this occurred during Kayla's five months of life! Since I fully anticipated being a single parent or at least being the main provider of my child's needs in the not-too-distant future, I was making arrangements so Kayla would have all the advantages I had been afforded.

A few weeks after Kayla's death, before I had even returned to work on September 30, 1996, I contacted a support group. The woman I spoke with, the founder of the Miscarriage, Infant Death, and Stillbirth group (MIS), was so patient and kind on the telephone. I went to three meetings and found them extremely helpful. I learned from others that very often following the death of a child, women sometimes experience a miscarriage. Although disheartening, at least I felt prepared and, thus, would not be *Seeking professional support helped save me.* caught totally off guard should that additional loss happen to be in my future. My husband and I went to another support group once. I did not feel as comfortable in that group because people had lost children of all ages. When an older child dies, the parents are able to talk about what happened throughout the years, favorite holidays, and other things to which I had no experience. The MIS group included women who had experienced loss from the earliest stages of pregnancy, so we were able to talk about the brief lives of our children had, as well as of the future plans and the expectations we had for them.

What was so surprising to me was that I continued to receive hospital bills from the first hospital up to one year after Kayla's death. Dealing with the insurance company was a nightmare, and I began to feel harassed by the hospital although she was there at most for four hours. Children's Hospital never sent me a bill for which I am truly grateful although Kayla was there for three days and the cost of her care was, no doubt, enormous. I had personally informed the hospital staff of Kayla's death soon after and learned they were already aware. Other contractual organizations sent bills as well. One of the bills from the first hospital happened to arrive on the six-month anniversary of Kayla's death—February 12, 1997—and another just before Mother's

Day. Of course, I am fully aware of the bills being computer-generated, but human beings are the ones to input the information into the computer system. The staff at Children's Hospital behaved in a thoroughly sensitive manner, so it obviously can be done. Although I understand that hospitals need to get paid for their services, they do not seem to understand how difficult breathing becomes after such a significant loss, nor do they seem to care. With all I was dealing with, it seems to me the insurance company could have been contacted directly by the hospital. For weeks, I called the insurance company and finally the bills were paid. I had to do all of the advocating myself and wish that they could have attempted to appreciate what I had gone through and billed the insurance company directly instead of having me receive the bills and forward them myself.

Kayla died in September, my husband moved out in October, and I started a new job in November. I see children as my ministry and ensuring they have bright futures as part of my mission. I felt I was a darn good child welfare social worker, but after Kayla died, I felt that I could no longer adequately advocate for the birth parents that I was responsible for providing services. Although some of them indeed "turn their lives around," I was no longer able to adequately advocate for parents who had abused and neglected their children while still having a chance to be reunified with them. After all, I never abused or neglected my child yet I had no opportunity to be with her. One of my "friends" did not understand my inability to continue to do this type of work at that point in my life. The defining moment for me was when a scheduled visit was to occur. The child waited for forty-five minutes, and I told the foster mother she could leave after the birth mother had not arrived or called. Eventually the birth mother did show up and was angry that the visit would not occur. She threatened to inform the judge, but this fell on deaf ears as court appearances and testifying never intimidated me. My first thought was, *"If I had five minutes to be with Kayla, I certainly would not be late."* I was aware that I was no longer non-judgmental and thus an immediate change was required as the birth parents, too, deserve professional treatment.

I began working at Catholic Charities on November 18, 1996, in the Pregnancy and Adoptions Program. My supervisor soon learned how openly I share my business and said, *"You have no problem with self disclosure."* In this program, I was responsible for working with birth mothers considering making an adoption plan. I felt this was indeed a good fit for me. I was able to empathize with them because I knew firsthand how paralyzing it can be to make difficult decisions about your child, as well as what it is like to face the future without your child. I could also relate to adoptive parents, many of whom had fertility issues, desperately wanting to parent while dealing with the disappointment of being unable to have children "naturally." That job seemed an ideal match, not only due to the nature of my work, but also because of the support of the staff and the fact that I was working with a Christian organization. However, I found it very difficult to meet my financial obligations and after nearly three years, began working for the Child and Family Services Agency in the Adoptions Unit on July 6, 1999. From there, I moved to South Washington/West of the River Family Strengthening Collaborative on July 3, 2000. Unfortunately, supervising did not agree with me at that point in my career, so I moved to work as a foster parent coordinator at [unnamed agency], a non-profit foster care agency, on July 2, 2001. After working there for ten years, I was called into a meeting. [The current director] started the conversation by saying, *"This is hard."* Before she uttered another word, I said, *"Lord, please help me to accept whatever is to come."* I was unceremoniously told that my salary would be cut by $40,000 and it was "not personal." I had just purchased a second home on March 23, 2011.

What was I to do? I went into the bathroom and called my best friend. She was incredulous. My parents were out of town, but I called my mother and said that I might need help with my mortgage payment. On July 27, 2011, I sent a memorandum to the President and CEO of the company requesting a meeting to address my decrease in hours. I stated

I have been employed by [unnamed agency] since July 2, 2001 and am very proud of the accomplishments I have made throughout the years. All of my performance reviews have been outstanding and it has always been recommended that I receive the largest percentage available as an increase in salary. [The former director] stated several times that she had received many compliments on the home studies I have written throughout the years and [a foster father] recently submitted a glowing letter on my behalf. During my 9:00 a.m. meeting with [the current director] on Monday, July 25, 2011, I was told that my work has always been "stellar."

Needless to say, I was devastated and blindsided to learn during that meeting that my employment status has been reduced to part-time. I failed to ask if furloughs had been considered as the financial burden would then have been shared by all as was the case in raising the cost of the health insurance while decreasing the benefits. After eight (8) months, it appears my job may be in jeopardy as at that time it will be reevaluated as to whether my position is even needed. As a single mother of two young children, ages 14 and 8, both having physical and emotional challenges, it will be much more difficult for me to make ends meet. However, know that I am truly blessed to have a job with health insurance and thank you tremendously for that ongoing benefit!

I was told that my hours were being decreased due to the agency being in the red due to a lack of placements being made. It seems ironic, then, that someone who lives in another state would be paid to travel to update a foster home when we inherited two from [another foster care agency]. When I began working at [unnamed agency], I was involved in placements, but that task was removed from me without explanation around 2002. I reminded [the current director] that I have licensed foster homes—we currently have eleven (11) slots available—and thus I had done what I was hired to do. I was told that even if we do increase our placements, I would not even be considered for full-time status. I responded that it appeared the two were related although I was not responsible for placements. When I spoke to [a manager at another agency] on July 13, 2011 during our monthly Training Resources Committee meeting, I learned that [unnamed agency] has repeatedly only accepted the placements of "easy" children who are classified as traditional. Again, it appears that we have slots available yet they are not being utilized.

Three people have been hired to recruit additional foster homes since approximately 2007 as it was believed that this should have a concentrated focus. It is impossible to license foster homes if there are few to license. I was told that, on average, I have licensed ten (10) foster homes annually, but will now be required to license fifteen (15) while working fewer hours. I am certainly willing to do all that is required in licensing foster homes as quickly as possible although the duration in licensing will unavoidably increase with the implementation of the [new] home study model.

Please note that I am committed to the work that I do and the families we serve by coming in most Sundays – and never seeking any type of compensation – to ensure [unnamed agency's] children are safe and the foster families are supported and appreciated. In order to successfully accomplish this, I had previously organized the annual "Foster Parent Speak-Out" in order to address grievances, listen to suggestions, and ensure there was no miscommunication. I had suggested that more be done to retain the excellent foster parents. As we are part of the [church], I was admonished for mentioning God or blessings although both are very instrumental to the African-American community which is the race most greatly represented among our foster parent community.

I will continue to be a team player which is, in part, evident by my donation of items for the [unnamed agency's] day care center on Friday, July 22, 2011. As the parent of a deceased child, I know that God will take care of me and my family as He has done in the past, is doing in the present, and will continue to do in the future. Proverbs 3:5-6 and Romans 8:28 say, respectively,

"Trust in the LORD with all thine heart; and lean not unto thine own understanding. In all thy ways acknowledge Him, and He shall direct thy paths."

"And we know that all things work together for good to them that love God, to them who are the called according to His purpose."

Although I am away August 1 through August 3, I would greatly appreciate a meeting with you, at your earliest convenience, to discuss my employment status.

Although I received that devastating news on Monday, July 25, 2011, I spoke to my former supervisor at For Love of Children the following day about something completely unrelated to my dilemma. After addressing the reason she contacted me, I shared my plight. Remarkably, she had a job available! I interviewed on Thursday, July 28, 2011 and the job was offered to me the following day. I submitted my resignation on Friday, July 29, 2011 and began my new employment at MENTOR Maryland on August 8, 2011 although I continued to work at [unnamed agency] until Wednesday, August 31, 2011. It appears that I have had many successive losses, but God is always with me, and I try to move to where He would have me. It is ONLY Him to be the One to have a job lined up for me although I had not been looking and did not know that I would need one.

When things get really tough for me, I can always talk to God. I must remind myself that He hears all, but answers in His time. Sometimes God says, *"No,"* and at other times, He is working behind the scenes for our benefit. I recall Minister Joyce Meyer saying, *"God is not late, but He's not early either."* There are so many positive and uplifting things that have happened to me that I know it could only have been orchestrated by Him. I thank God that I always have Someone to Whom to turn.

I Thought of You with Love Today
author unknown

I thought of you with love today, but that is nothing new.
I thought about you yesterday, and the day before that, too.
I think of you in silence, I often say your name,
But all I have is memories and your picture in a frame.
Your memory is my keepsake, with which I'll never part.
God has you in His keeping, I have you in my heart.
I shed tears for what might have been, a million times I've cried.
If love alone could have saved you, you never would have died.
In life I loved you dearly, in death I love you still,
In my heart you hold a place no one could ever fill.
It broke my heart to lose you, but you didn't go alone,
For part of me went with you, the day God took you Home.

WAYS TO REMEMBER
MY FIRST CHILD

"Little deeds of kindness, little words of love, help to make earth happy, like the heaven above." ~Julia Fletcher Carney

My birthday is two days before Kayla's birthday. My parents took me to a very nice restaurant for dinner in March 1997. They gave me the most wonderfully unique present. Kayla's room had rocking horses stenciled just under the ceiling, which my father had taken the time to do precisely. My mother and I put rocking horses on our Christmas tree the year Kayla died. My father took one of the rocking horses to a jeweler and had a pendant designed for me. The jeweler traveled to New York and found a horse. He added a rocker and put Kayla's name under that. The horse even has a diamond in his eye. It is so beautiful and precious – like Kayla. I continue to get

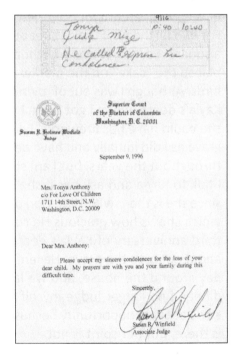

complements of it to this day. I wear my gift always and feel "naked" if I remove it to wear a different necklace. I was also touched because it was solely my father's idea. He began working on it in January 1997, and picked it up about three weeks before my birthday. I still get emotional when I think of my father's insight, planning, compassion, and the gift itself.

On June 21, 2011, I got a rocking horse tattoo on my left ankle. When a doctor noticed it, I said, "I'm not really a tattoo person." He replied, "But you are a memory person."

I used to go to Kayla's grave often. Several of my friends have gone to see the marker, and my former mother-in-law even called to tell me how nice it was. I felt I needed to go there at least for all of the first holidays and even went three days in a row once – my birthday, Easter, and Kayla's birthday. My mother and I have taken balloons, cards, Easter basket, a rabbit on a stick whose ears turned in the wind, a Christmas wreath, and even a small Christmas tree. For two birthdays, I took a suet block bird seed that was formed into a square. For me, it was a birthday cake to Kayla. I took candles and placed the "cake" on the marker so that she could be visited by the birds. Although I was out of town for the first Fourth of July following Kayla's death, when I got back, I took sparklers to her grave so that she could have her fireworks. I do not feel as obligated to go to the grave as I did initially and have decreased the frequency of my visits throughout the years, but I am still comforted by going. Sometimes I talk to Kayla and ask her if she can get answers from God for me since she is there with Him. God understands I have a long way to go, which shows how gracious He continues to be towards me. On the third anniversary of Kayla's death, I did not feel the same urgency about going to the grave. Haven, my daughter, and I had a leisurely day around the house, and we later, with my parents, went out to dinner. I no longer judge myself as a "bad mother" if I do not visit Kayla at every opportunity because as Christians can attest, her body is there, but her spirit is not.

Of course, I still have Kayla's pictures around and talk about her to others. One person told me that by keeping her picture on my mantle, I had developed a shrine to her and was making it more "difficult" on myself. Needless to say, I disagreed and her photos remain. I am truly grateful to those who mention Kayla openly themselves. I attended a few support groups and had gone to an annual Catholic mass in honor of deceased children until I learned they did not want non-Catholics to accept communion. I have completed Kayla's photo album and the first Christmas following her death, I mailed a picture of Kayla and a poem to all of my family and friends.

During an Easter service where I was working at the time, which happened to be two days after Kayla's first birthday, I got up to share the joy of Kayla and how people have supported me following her death. I started not to speak because people did not know me or Kayla, as I was a very new employee, but my heart was pounding out of my chest. I told God that if a friend of mine shared a testimony, then I would. What do you think happened?! This friend got up to speak! I had no

Openly sharing about my daughter helps to keep her memory alive.

choice then, and now am very glad that I did. The Development Office interviewed me several days later and wrote a story about my experience to send to donors! It was very tastefully done and a way to raise money for needy children within the agency. The Executive Director of the agency said that he had gotten more positive comments on that story than any other. For those employees that requested, they could receive a copy of the poem. God's word has certainly gotten out...and will continue to!

Soon after Kayla died, I felt that I needed to gather all of the information about her life that was available. I requested the medical records from the hospital where she was born, the pediatrician's office, the two hospitals in which she was transported, and even the autopsy results. For the longest time, I did not even think that an autopsy had been completed because it took so long to arrive, and I had to again personally talk to the medical examiner on the telephone. When I did see some of the medical records, it hit me pretty hard the first time I saw the word "expired." As a social worker, it was surreal to be the client being interviewed by a social worker. A child protective service report and police report were conducted for further investigation. My husband and I were said to be "very distressed" which was obviously appropriate, but it is now humbling to know that we were being assessed as I had done numerous times of others. It was also said, "Appropriate grieving noted. Mom and Dad... very tearful, asked appropriate questions and kept updated on status."

Since 1991, I have had personalized tags on my car. After Kayla died, I put "Symonne" on my tags as "Kayla" was unavailable. I kept that tag about two years until I began to feel that I needed a change as I was continuing to heal so I let that tag go. In June 1999, I changed my tag to "SERVHIM." Healing can certainly take place in unexpected ways, but as long as you continue to heal and to grow, you can feel free to do it in your own way and at your own pace.

Other things I did to keep Kayla's memory alive were to have a dedication played on the radio and a memoriam placed in the newspaper on her birthday and the anniversary of her death. This ritual continued for ten years. I am on the Advisory Committee for the Center for Infant ***God looks for availability, not ability.*** and Child Loss and attend their annual memorial service in December which can be a difficult time for many bereaved parents. I am very involved in assisting other bereaved parents in any way that I can and offer "peer counseling" to those who desire it. I have begun my organization, Kayla's Village, to keep her memory alive and to help parents and social service professionals. It has been said, *"God's plan for our life is bigger than our own."* Be careful when you pray the Prayer of Jabez, as it says in 1Chronicles 4:10,

> And Jabez called on the God of Israel, saying, Oh that thou wouldest bless me indeed, and enlarge my coast, and that thine hand might be with me, and that thou wouldest keep me from evil, that it may not grieve me! And God granted him that which he requested.

When people tell me how good I look and that I look like I am doing well, I say that is more evidence of how good God is. I am not strong, but rather, His strength manifests itself through ***"Blessed are they that mourn for they shall be comforted. ~Matthew 5:4*** me. I am stronger than I ever wanted to be, but see absolutely nothing wrong with having been "weak and ignorant." I am humbly trying to learn and do God's will.

Christmas in Heaven
by Wanda Bencke

I see the countless Christmas trees around the world below
With tiny lights like Heaven's stars reflecting on the snow.
The sight is so spectacular, please wipe away that tear
For I am spending Christmas with Jesus Christ this year.
I hear the many Christmas songs that people hold so dear
But the sounds of music can't compare with the Christmas
choir up here.
I have no words to tell you of the joy their voices bring
For it is beyond description to hear the angels sing.
I know how much you miss me because I am still near
But I am spending Christmas with Jesus Christ this year.
I can't tell you of the splendor or the peace here in this place
Can you just imagine Christmas with our Savior face-to-face?
I'll ask Him to lift your spirit as I am reminded of your love
So then pray for one another as you lift your eyes above.
Please let your hearts be joyful and let your spirit sing
I am spending Christmas in Heaven...walking with the King.

INSPIRATIONAL HAPPENINGS

"A newborn chick doesn't know it's alive until its world begins to crumble. What seems like the collapse of your universe may be just an exciting beginning." ~Thomas Nelson

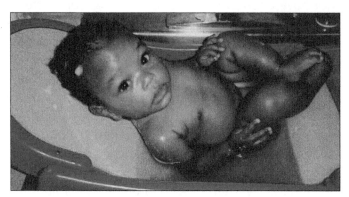

There was a time after my separation when I felt that I might not be ready to be in a relationship because I looked at it as another potential loss. I had gained much from being a mother, but little from being a wife. Thus, in November 1996, I began considering all of my options to become a mother again via having sexual intercourse, artificial insemination, foster care, and adoption. I knew that I eventually wanted another birth child in part to resolve my issue around not being able finalize my breastfeeding plan (and, yes, I am aware that adopted children can be breastfeed), but I had told myself that I would wait one year before making any major decisions. Since we are all brothers- and sisters-in-Christ, I knew I was "related" to any child that I would adopt long before I ever met my child. A year after

Kayla's death seemed like a good gauge because I would have been through all the "firsts" and would have had some time to heal. My therapist supported my timeframe.

I explored a "foster-to-adopt" program because I wanted an infant, which usually meant a long wait. My mother went to an information meeting with me. I was not really discouraged, but knew I wanted a child to remain with me permanently as the possibility of a foster child leaving my home was great. In this arena, I was clearly a potential parent and not a social worker. As a result, I decided to get artificially inseminated. I had talked to both my gynecologist and pediatrician and had requested information from two clinics. I chose to be inseminated by an unknown donor because if I was going to be a single parent, I wanted to be one in the total sense of the word. There would be no need for anyone to be involved since the child would not have been the product of a loving, committed relationship. My mother was not interested in helping to choose the donor, but she had agreed to be with me when I had the procedure done.

August 7, 1997, was typical of all of my days during that time. I was feeling sorry for myself with the impending first anniversary of Kayla's death, and the divorce going nowhere. I was always crying and on my knees asking the Lord, *"Please reveal to me what You want me to know."* I was reminded that I need not pressure myself into knowing the answers for my life because God knows them all. What a relief!

Miraculously, I learned of a child being available for adoption almost accidentally on August 8, 1997, about one month shy of my self-imposed goal date. A birth mother had wanted to make an adoption plan for her nearly three-month-old daughter, Briana. Immediately, within my spirit, I knew this was the path for me instead of artificial insemination. My father had purchased a cell phone for me due to the situation that had occurred with Kayla. They were not nearly a fifth appendage in 1997 as in today's world. I had been instructed to use it only in emergencies. When my spirit spoke to me, I called my father saying, *"This IS an emergency! I think I have just met my daughter!"* He was not very enthusiastic. My father was actively grieving as were we all. So, began the process of adoption of this baby.

On August 15, 1997, I was typing as I listened to the soundtrack of The Preacher's Wife, easily my favorite CD. Many of the songs seemed to minister to me, and I began to cry and to feel at peace. It was at this time that the Lord told me that Briana was my daughter, but immediately, my human side began to doubt. I tried to shake it off – like the song sung at Kayla's Homegoing Service – and told my supervisor that this child was mine as I needed to verbalize my faith to others. I later told my mother I was claiming this child as mine, and she thought that I must have gotten information from the agency. I said, *"No, I talked to Someone a little higher than that."* My mother said, *"How can you claim her when the mother hasn't signed the relinquishment papers?"* I replied, *"I'm claiming her in the name of the Lord."*

That same month, my parents and I went to Myrtle Beach, South Carolina, with my church. I called the social worker to check on the status of the adoption proceedings. She said that the birth mother had changed her mind and decided to parent her daughter. Honestly, I was fine with that decision because as a mother, I completely understood wanting to be with my child. After all, the child had yet to be placed with me. Others thought I would be disappointed, but I did not feel I had any *I missed parenting, but not being in a relationship. Adoption was a viable option!* right to be that selfish. God knows the beginning from the end and had told me the child was mine. Perhaps, that is why I did not fret. Of course, I was not thinking at the time that Briana would come to me, but I also did not harbor any bitterness or anger about the mother's change of heart. My father said, *"I hear we're not getting the baby,"* which really meant a lot to me because I knew then that he supported my decision to adopt. He had previously said that adopting a child would not be the same, but I reminded him that no matter how many children I had by birth, it would not be the same *AND* was not supposed to be regardless of how a child joins the family because all people are individuals. My father's acceptance of my potential new daughter was a great encouragement to me, even though it appeared that this would not be the particular child for me. The social worker said that the birth mother decided to have her daughter returned to her. I rationalized that if the birth mother felt she could parent her child to adulthood, I would pray for her to be successful in that decision. Although it was anticipated that I would be disappointed, I was actually fine with her decision because my thought was, *"If I were able to be with my daughter, then that is where I would want her to be."* Immediately, however, I felt that I had misread God's revelation and doubt crept in that Briana was to become my daughter.

When I had found out about Briana being in need of an adoptive placement, I had expected everything to be "smooth sailing." I received a message from God that she would be placed with me, but then I began to doubt. The birth mother had not signed any legal documents. She contacted the social worker and informed her that her family had agreed to help her to raise her child. I knew that she and the social worker were to meet and called to hear the outcome while I was on vacation in Myrtle Beach, South Carolina.

When I returned from my vacation, the social worker said that she needed to talk to me. She told me that the birth mother was coming in for a meeting, but she was not bringing the baby with her. I felt like I could not keep going through these ups and downs of possibilities and losses. A few days later, following the meeting, the birth mother said that things were not working out as she had anticipated and that she wanted to follow through with making an adoption plan. At that moment, I knew that I had been wrong not to trust God. He had told me that Briana was mine, but I was looking at the situation around me instead of looking steadfastly towards God. Briana was again placed into her previous foster home.

The birth mother carefully considered her decision and on August 25, 1997, Briana was back in the same pre-adoptive home! I knew the moment that information was shared with me that beyond any shadow of any doubt, I had not misinterpreted God's message, but rather I had not been faithful in my trust of Him. Indeed, THIS was to be my child. There were many obstacles, but they were to be overcome. The birth mother had canceled two appointments to help choose the adoptive family because she found it too difficult. She expressed what qualities were most important to her and had no problem with her daughter being raised by a single female. The social worker shared information with the birth mother about me, and she said that I sounded nice. I have so much respect for the birth mother, who was in college and realized she did not have the family support she needed to raise a child while fulfilling her goals. Neither the birth father, nor his family was supportive, so she really struggled with her decision. The birth mother agreed to meet me, and I was so excited. I had planned to give her a frame as a gift, symbolizing my commitment to continue sending updates to her throughout the years. However, we were both in the building at the same time, but she could not bring herself to meet the woman who would parent the daughter she loved so dearly. The relinquishment papers were signed on September 19, 1997, and I was chosen on October 1, 1997.

The name the birth mother gave, *"Briana Amari,"* was really a beautiful name, and I had considered keeping it. I have a cousin named Briana. I did not think Briana Anthony had a smooth flow, so I began exploring other possibilities. I often saw the name "Heaven" on street signs, in the newspaper, and worked with a birth mother who had given it as a middle name to her child as the treatment center had been a haven for her. One person thought the name was too close to "heaven," and another questioned what "possessed" me to give her that name. Some do not like it while others love it. I decided I was going to name my daughter *"Briana"* because I always wanted her to be safe (in light of Kayla's accident) and secure (sometimes a greater struggle in single parent and possibly adoptive households). At church, we sang "safe and secure from all alarms" and when visiting a hospitalized church member, I saw a sign that said "Safe to Secure Valuables." I prayed for guidance one night, and the very next morning on the cover of <u>Parade</u> magazine was an article about a "haven" for abused animals. The Lord knows that I require much confirmation, and He was giving it to me left and right! I hyphenated her middle name because her birth mother named her "Briana" (meaning strength and virtue), and I also wanted her to have the middle name of "Symonne." My thinking was that although Kayla and Haven could not share a life, they could share a name. I used "Symonne" in order to honor both of my children, and not in any way

I needed a way to have my two daughters connected.

attempt to replace Kayla. I also wanted Haven to know that since Symonne was "good enough" for my birth child, and because we are not generally identified by our middle names, I thought of her no differently. I chose to keep Anthony as my last name, although some people may think that it is a connection to my ex-husband it was a connection to Kayla that I was not ready to give up then. When my parents finally asked about the name I was going to use, they really liked "Briana," could tolerate "Haven," and had an issue with me using "Symonne." They did raise me to be an independent thinker, right?

The social worker told me in October 1997, that the birth mother and her mother came to the office. They missed Briana and wanted her back, although the birth mother's revocation period had expired. We later learned that she had relinquished to another agency who, then, should not have returned the child to her, which meant the current relinquishment was most likely invalid. The birth mother had said that the birth father was deceased, but later gave the name of a person who was very much alive. At this point, I was really ready to fight for her, although she had not yet been placed with me. Legally, the birth mother was no longer the legal mother. Although I was fully aware of how difficult the decision was for the birth mother, I was growing concerned about the constant fluctuations and possible instability of Briana's placement with her birth family. While driving home, I continually recalled the Lord telling me this child was mine. If I did not proceed as planned, what would that say about my faith? God would not bring me this far to leave me and so many obstacles had already been overcome. I did not want God to say, *"Now didn't I TELL you I had worked it out?"* After reflecting on the situation, I decided I would not fight the birth mother in court, if she sincerely wanted to parent her child as much as I wanted to adopt a child that had no home. However, I was not willing to give her up so easily if the maternal grandmother or maternal aunt would be the one parenting her. I could appreciate facing the future without my child, as well as what adoptive parents go through with the uncertainty and legal risk involved. The birth mother had once said that her mother did not really want them in the house and provided minimal support. We have no way of knowing if that statement was accurate or if that was a means to move toward making an adoption plan. The maternal aunt believed that Briana was with her paternal grandmother, yet did not call to check on her for the four months she was supposedly in that home. All of this was further confirmation to me about this child being mine because most other prospective adoptive families would probably be scared and ask to have a different child presented for placement. I prayed for strength to accept the Lord's will because *"While I'm trying to figure it out, God has already worked it out."* I saw the situation as having little to do with the birth mother and her child, but everything to do with Jesus and me. I fasted at various points in the process, which helped to strengthen my faith. One day, the song "We Haven't Finished Yet" made me cry joyfully because the Lord was reminding me that He was still working things out with and for me. Things are certainly done in His timing and not mine.

My mother and I attended a good friend's "mega church" on October 12, 1997. The minister said, *"A delay is not a denial"* and requested that whoever had legal troubles to come to the altar. I was dealing with the impending divorce and Haven's situation so I went down. I believe the Lord was encouraging me to keep the faith that I would indeed parent again. This ordeal was extremely hard on me, but my parents as well because they were trying to love this child from afar, but were understandably fearful of having to not hold a child they love in their arms. If things did not work out in my favor, my thought was that perhaps my parents would more readily embrace the idea of artificial insemination, since no one would have a right to the child but me. If Haven were eventually placed with me, I did not want to be perceived as having "taken" her from her birth mother. I wanted to have a relationship with the birth mother and had hoped she would give us her blessing. To some degree, my heart would break regardless of the outcome. I remember what it was like September 4, 1996, when Kayla was still on life support, and I believe the birth mother was possibly experiencing similar feelings—the painful reality that control is nowhere to be found and not having a clue how things would turn out. I thanked God that I was affiliated with an ethical agency who would do all they could for all birth parents. I would do the same if I was the social worker and not the adoptive parent. We would all have to live with ourselves after everything was said and done.

The social workers at both agencies which accepted the relinquishments met with the birth mother on October 29, 1997. After learning that her child might linger in foster care or be placed elsewhere, she admitted that she had lied by initially giving the name of her recently deceased cousin as the birth father. She gave an address for the birth father, which she had been involved with since junior high school, and stated that she did not believe he was interested in parenting because he was living with his cousin. She said she always wanted to make an adoption plan, but she was being pressured by her mother to keep the baby. I was relieved that she was actually at peace with her decision.

Thankfully, I was able to have a visit at my house with Haven on December 17, 1997. My mother came and brought her a pliable necklace in the shape of a Christmas tree with a face, arms, and legs. After she left, Haven and I went to visit Santa at the mall. The first picture did not turn out too well so the assistant agreed to take it again. Haven was smiling broadly and had a great day. Then, December 23, 1997, arrived and my daughter was placed with me! With her came the carrying seat the birth mother had provided. I will save that seat always, along with the clothes she was wearing. My father's birthday is Christmas Eve so being able to meet his second grandchild for the first time was a priceless gift. My mother and I had already bought Haven many presents and thankfully we could be able to give them to her.

After meeting her, many people comment on how much Haven looks like me. I confidently reply, "God *knows what He is doing.*" The social worker said Haven has her birth mother's eyes, which made me happy because that is certainly her most distinguishing feature noticed by the majority. In January 1998, I had a "Welcome Home, Haven" party in order to introduce her to all my family and friends. It was a potluck event, and the house was packed! A glorious time was had by all.

Haven has truly been a blessing. Yes, I was tired and often overwhelmed, but parenting was what I expected, and I think that I was somewhat prepared. Although I was certain she had stopped breathing the first night, it took us all time to adjust. My parents and I had called Haven by Kayla's name initially, but we worked very hard not to continually make that mistake.

On January 2, 1998, a friend I met through an in-home shopping service called and said she and her husband wanted to increase their tithing by helping someone in need. They chose me and agreed to give me $50.00 a month worth of baby items! I began to cry and my friend said, *"This is a gift from God, not us."* This arrangement lasted for about two years and truly, truly helped out this struggling single parent.

For Haven's first birthday, it was an unseasonably warm day. I had a party in the backyard and my father dressed up as a clown. Haven's theme is clowns just as Kayla's was rocking horses. He looked great and, although he is very reserved and quiet, he did a fantastic job interacting with everyone. There must have been 60 people in attendance and so many presents that I was overwhelmed by them all. Haven began walking eight days after her birthday and has been busy ever since.

The judge issued an order to show cause, scheduled for August 19, 1998, against the birth father, as he had not cooperated in relinquishing his parental rights. Remember, Haven had been my daughter since December 23, 1997. An order to show cause is one in which the party must explain the situation and show just cause why something should not happen. The court successfully contacted him, and he expressed an interest in parenting his daughter. I began to wonder whether the birth mother encouraged him to exert his parental rights, as they continued to maintain contact. The hearing was continued until September 21, 1998, in order to give the birth father the opportunity to state his case before the Court. The social worker visited the birth mother prior to that date in an attempt to gather more information and clarity. The birth mother was at work, but the grandmother expressed that she would have raised Briana and wanted a chance to say goodbye. I agreed to a visit *after* I received the final decree of adoption. During that entire period, however, I was very much a parent and not a social worker so it was extremely hard for me to accept that my daughter might be taken from my home and placed elsewhere.

When I decided to write a book, of course, I considered publishers. A friend suggested that I talk to someone that had successfully gotten his book published. This person felt that Xulon Press was the publishing company to utilize due to its reputation, packages available, opportunities, and because it was Christian-based. I explored the website and requested its free mailed information. Xulon had a contest for prospective authors. After my second submission, I was contacted because it was felt that my writing had promise. What encouragement and an ego booster! My writing that generated some interest was

Journeying from Loss to Blessing

My daughter, Kayla Symonne, was born on Palm Sunday, March 31, 1996 at 6:53 a.m. Sadly, on September 4, 1996, she was in a strangulation accident which led to cardiac and respiratory arrest. On Friday, September 6, 1996 at 6:53 p.m., I ended the life support.

After that, I did not think the sun would shine for me again. My husband and I separated one month following our daughter's death due to his issues, not the unexpected loss of our child. The divorce was finalized one year later.

I struggled with how to move forward while incorporating the loss of my daughter into my life. I was not ready to get into another relationship, but I missed parenting. Why not adopt?! My quest began.

I contacted an adoption agency to complete my required home study and learned of a girl who was voluntarily placed for adoption. I met with the social worker and learned of her history. The plan was moving forward quickly! I told my parents who were continuing to adjust to the loss of their granddaughter, but willingly supported me. Overtime, all of us became equally excited and anxious!

I received the call. The social worker said the birth mother had changed her mind, rescinded her relinquishment, and was going to parent instead. My father said, *"I guess we are not going to get the baby."* Honestly, I was **NOT** devastated. The child had not been placed with me. My response was, "I understand. If I had a chance to be with my child, I would." I was coming to the realization that "what God has for me is for me." There must be something God was protecting me from or some other plan He had in store.

One week later, I received another call from the social worker. The same birth mother—who had parented for three months of her daughter's life—realized she did not have the support needed to raise a child to adulthood and thus courageously returned the infant to the agency. She wanted to complete her education and sought that—and more—for her child. Was I still interested in having this child placed with me? Of course! Again, the birth mother had to sign the relinquishment papers—the "easy" part because the birth father had yet to sign anything. I was willing to take that risk. On December 23, 1997, my daughter, Haven Briana-Symonne, came home to me. I decided to include "Symonne" in Haven's name because although she could not share a life with her sister, they could share a name. I also wanted Haven to know that if that name were good enough for a birth child, she would know I felt no differently about her joining the family via adoption. In January 1998, we had a "Welcome Home, Haven" party.

Legally, the birth father had to be contacted. Eight months after Haven was placed with me, he decided he wanted to parent. **NOW** I was devastated! My child had tubes put in her ears when she was only eleven months old due to frequent and severe ear infections. I saw her take her first steps. I fed her homemade baby food. We were bonded. I was more than a caretaker. Where had this man been for the past year?

I was clearly my child's mother at that point. What was I to do? Pray!

The court hearing did not take place because the birth father said he was not aware of the proceedings and thus could not be present. One month later, after not showing up for the second time, his parental rights were terminated. After about one week, on September 27, 1998, my daughter was "legally" mine. Time for another party!

My daughter is now fourteen years old and doing extremely well in school. She has traveled internationally several times and is a proud big sister to her eight-year-old brother, Christian. I must be doing something right by focusing on the positives of adoption as my son has said, *"I want to be adopted."* My daughter, being a typical teen, has had some challenges with me, but she also said, *"I can't imagine not being born to you."*

There is a moral to my story. No matter how dim the future seems, be open to God's leading and He will comfort you and give you the desires of your heart. Once that does occur, be sure to thank Him for all He has done.

Drinking from my Saucer
by John Paul Moore

I've never made a fortune
and it's probably too late now.
But I don't worry about that much,
I'm happy anyhow.

And as I go along life's way,
I'm reaping better than I sowed.
I'm drinking from my saucer,
'Cause my cup has overflowed.

I haven't got a lot of riches,
and sometimes the going's tough.
But I've got loved ones around me,
and that makes me rich enough.

I thank God for His blessings,
and the mercies He's bestowed.
I'm drinking from my saucer,
'cause my cup has overflowed.

I remember times when things went wrong,
My faith wore somewhat thin.
But all at once the dark clouds broke,
and the sun peeped through again.

So, God, help me not to gripe about
the tough rows that I've hoed.
I'm drinking from my saucer,
'Cause my cup has overflowed.

If God gives me strength and courage,
when the way grows steep and rough.
I'll not ask for other blessings,
I'm already blessed enough.

And may I never be too busy,
to help others bear their loads.
Then I'll keep drinking from my saucer,
'cause my cup has overflowed.

ANOTHER ROLLERCOASTER

"It is during our times of greatest challenges that we receive our most profound revelations – and our clearest vision."
~Michael Norwood

I believe Haven was placed into my home with an undiagnosed ear infection. The pediatric nurse only became aware of the ear infection when they looked into her years. Haven's pleasant, easygoing, and engaging personality were not affected one iota! She had to be closely monitored and receive antibiotics for three months beginning the month after her placement. Tubes were placed in both of her ears when she was only 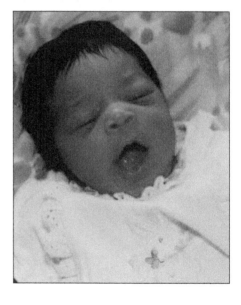 eleven months old due to the excessive build up of fluid. With all of the observing, dispensing of medications as the antibiotics led to a yeast infection, and time spent together, I very much felt confident being her mother.

Although I honestly trusted that the social worker had done all she could regarding the child, birth parents, and myself, I still wondered if she would be taken from me after bonding with her as my daughter for eight months. I was indeed fearful and began to pray. I did not talk to my parents about the impending situation because I did not want them to worry and ask me questions I was unable to answer.

The social worker called on September 21, 1998, and asked to speak to "Haven Anthony." I said, "It's finalized?!" She said everyone was sworn in, "grilled," and the proceedings were over pretty quickly as the birth father did not appear. Haven and I went out to dinner to celebrate and "officially" establish ourselves as a family. We had a party to recognize that Haven was "legal." I even had the waitress take a picture of us to commemorate the day. Actually, the Order of Adoption Decree was signed on September 27, 1998, so this is the date we now celebrate. It has always been said, *"Don't wait until the battle is over, we can rejoice now!"* I often think I know the answers, but only God really knows. He prevailed yet again.

After having experienced the depths of pain and despair, I was able to experience the other end of the spectrum with joy that nearly took my breath away. I would again parent!

Will the Circle Be Unbroken
by Charles H. Gabriel

There are loved ones in the glory,
Whose dear forms you often miss;
When you close your earthly story,
Will you join them in their bliss?

In the joyous days of childhood,
Oft they told of wondrous love,
Pointed to the dying Savior;
Now they dwell with Him above.

You can picture happy gath'rings
'Round the fireside long ago,
And you think of tearful partings,
When they left you here below.

A SURPRISE BLESSING

"Joy is the infallible sign of the presence of God."
~Pierre Teilhard de Chardin

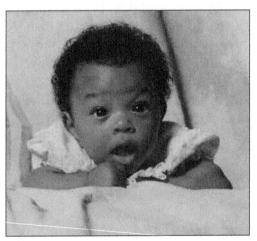

After my divorce was finalized on February 17, 1998, I was very comfortable being a single parent to my new daughter. Then, in July 1998, I began to have romantic feelings for a friend who had been interested in me for twenty-years. In retrospect, I believe I was vulnerable and wanted secure a father for my child. However, at that time, I reflected on that fact that he had been a platonic friend for many years, visited the hospital following Kayla's accident, attended the homegoing service, and supported me during my separation and divorce. He was comfortable. We married on October 27, 2001.

I now realize that I did not know him well, but rather merely knew him a long time. I had mistakenly shown him my "letter to

God" in which I outlined the qualities I was looking for in a mate. This person knew what to say and do to get me, but could not do what was needed to keep me. He and several of his friends think I "used" him to have another biological child, but that is sincerely untrue.

We began having problems very early in the marriage and now I will admit that we had discussed calling off the wedding, but I was not strong enough to do that at the time. He packed up his things to move from the home four months after the marriage, but I was not ready to announce to the world that this marriage, too, would not last. However, on January 18, 2002, our son was conceived.

When my former husband packed to move from the house, I was unaware that I was pregnant. My menstrual cycle did not begin as expected, but I attributed it to stress. After all, I was thirty-five years old and thought surely I knew how to "avoid" getting pregnant. The following month, I took a home pregnancy test and my announcement was, *"Look at what we have to deal with."*

For about two weeks, I felt fine. When I was less than two months pregnant, the uncontrollable vomiting, known as hyper emesis, began. I was so much worse than when I was pregnant with Kayla. Over time, at least five antidepressants were tried, but they aggravated the vomiting. I was hospitalized twice as I quickly lost thirteen pounds. I was given intravenous fluids at home with a nurse visiting every three days in order to move the line. During one night I was able to get a few hours of sleep, the line clogged so I had to be transported to the hospital by my mother in order to have some type of medication inserted in an attempt to open the line. To the nurse's surprise, it worked! I was given an apparatus that included an alarm so when the fluids were low, I would be awakened from my fitful rest so that I could change the bag of fluids. That seemed like an acceptable solution, but it was only temporary. As my vomiting did not appear to subside at all—there was one day I clearly recall vomiting seven times violently and had nothing to regurgitate but bile—it was suggested that I have a peripherally inserted central catheter (PICC line) inserted so that I would no longer be required to have the traditional IV line moved every three days to avoid infection. This was considered surgery so another visit to the hospital. I was so completely dehydrated that I was not certain I could endure the pain. My mother had to leave the room and one of the nurses came over to stroke my hair. The other nurse had to repeatedly twist the line in an attempt to get it into my shrunken vein. The PICC line was inserted the entire length of my right arm so that the fluid would be deposited directly into my chest. This could be left in place for weeks. However, prior to being considered successful surgery, I needed an x-ray to verify that the PICC line was in its proper place and had not gone into my neck. Thankfully, it had traveled to its proper destination.

Finally it seemed as though there would no longer be a need for me to be "violated" so often. Another hurdle had been overcome. About one week after the surgery, my arm began to hurt. I called the number that was left as I was told to get in touch with someone if any complications arose. I was told to move my arm in specific patterns because the line was probably resting on a vein. After no relief, the nurse was called and told to make a home visit to assess. When she saw my arm, she became alarmed and could not rule out an infection. I needed to have the PICC line removed immediately and reinserted in my left arm. I informed the nurse and most likely had to sign some type of waiver, but recall telling her, *"Regardless of what happens, if you take the line out, I will NOT have it reinserted."* The nurse removed the PICC line and there was no further at-home medical intervention.

It is an understatement to say that I was miserable. Friends would visit and would witness my vomiting episodes. One was not "grossed out," but rather came to sit next to me and rub my back during a particularly painful event. There was little I could do to bring myself any peace or comfort. I clearly recollect, however, when I was eleven weeks, six days pregnant, I was in the bathtub and called my best friend. I told her I did not think I would be able to

I was thinking I might miscarry—or even terminate the pregnancy.

continue the pregnancy. She wisely misrepresented information when she said that she believed you could not terminate a pregnancy after twelve weeks. I was not in a position to do any research and certainly knew I was not able to make a decision of that magnitude overnight. Instead, I would lie on the living room sofa most often with my mother – who stayed in the home for one month until I went to stay with my parents for two weeks – across the room on the loveseat. My mother admits that she was angry with God because He had already taken Kayla from us and now she had to see her child suffer so greatly. Christians are very aware that Christ suffered ultimately on the cross while His Father had to witness what Jesus had to endure. Still, *"We are not on the same level as Jesus."* I would repeatedly tell God that if I was going to die as a result of all of this suffering, please take me immediately and quickly. I believe I was passively suicidal.

Although I physically hurt my entire pregnancy and never felt well, the hyper emesis did subside when I was perhaps five months pregnant. I had put on the thirteen pounds that I initially lost and by the time I delivered my son, I had put on another three pounds. Due to the reality that I had not put on weight as anticipated, I had to have a Level II sonogram to ensure that the baby was developing appropriately. I took Haven, age five at the time, to the sonogram so that *"I'm Gonna Be Ready" by Yolanda Adams was God speaking directly to me.* she could learn more about adoption. She could see the baby instead of me and then we could talk about how she was in her birth mother and once she was born, she eventually came to live with me. When the technician said that I had a "take home baby" meaning that he would be over the preferred five and a half pounds, I thanked God and knew there was nothing for me to fear.

Ignorantly, I thought all pregnancy problems were behind me. I had been through enough, right? The nurse called. She said that my glucose test was 137 and at 139, the mother has gestational diabetes. I climbed into my bed and cried uncontrollably. My mother said, *"It's just getting to be too much, huh?"* I had been eating a great deal of fresh fruit because I thought I was doing the best for my unborn child. I stopped immediately. I had to have my blood drawn three times over several hours to see if, indeed, I did have gestational diabetes. God was faithful yet again because the test for diabetes was negative! I am not able to express how grateful I was for that news!

About two weeks prior to my delivery, I began to have contractions. My husband took me to the hospital, but they would not allow Haven into the room due to her age. My parents picked her up. After some testing, I was sent home. I was told to report to my obstetrician after several days and they were surprised to see me still pregnant. It was a false alarm and I felt as well as I had after the vomiting had ceased.

My parents and Haven's godmother went on a cruise. I arranged for my cousin and Haven's other godmother to come to the house to watch Haven if I went into labor while they were away. I did not feel well and assured Haven that if I were not home when she woke up in the morning, her godmother would be with her and I would call her as soon as I could. I called my cousin around 10:30 p.m. and told her I needed her to come to the house. She excitedly said, *"It's time?"* because she most likely did not think her services would be utilized. My cousin arrived and off to the hospital we went. Again, I had dilated to four centimeters. I was instructed to empty my bladder. When I got into the bed, more fluid came out. The nurse insisted I must have urinated on myself, but I disagreed. She tested the fluid and discovered my water had broken. The vomiting started again. I had an epidural. The doctor was called in and after merely three pushes and no episiotomy, Christian Isaiah Logan was born on Monday, October 14, 2002 at 2:34 a.m. My due date had been October 18 and he weighed a miraculous eight pounds.

Maurette Brown Clark sings, "The impossible is God's chance to work a miracle."

MEMORIALS

"I sometimes find it half a sin, to put to words the grief I feel,
For words like nature half reveal and half conceal the soul
within." ~Alfred Tennyson

*T*he death announcement in <u>The Washington Post</u> was

September 10, 1996
On September 6, 1996, at Children's Hospital, loving daughter of
Tonya and Charles Anthony; paternal great granddaughter of Earth
and Allen Hall and Lupearl Davis; paternal granddaughter of Carolyn
and Cleo Davis, Sr.; maternal granddaughter of Betty and Leonard
Maiden. Also survived by a host of other relatives and friends. From 7

to 9 p.m. Tuesday, September 10, friends may visit with the family at Trinity AME Zion Church, 3505 16th Street, N.W., where services will be Held at 11 a.m. on Wednesday, September 11. Internment Lincoln Memorial Cemetery. In lieu of Flowers, family requests memorial contributions be made to Pediatric Intensive Care Unit of Children's Hospital, 111 Michigan Avenue, N.W., Washington, D.C. 20010.

For ten years, I had a memorial played on Howard University's radio station each birthday and anniversary of Kayla's death as well as a submission in The Washington Post. The newspaper submission follow:

March 31, 1997
We were blessed with our baby for awhile so He trusted us with His precious child.
You were baptized with many at your side, all who witnessed know God will provide.
Death is God's blessing for jobs well done and He'll guide us until our time's come.
God has revealed to us that all is well as you'll never know pains some can tell.
As we all know, God makes no mistakes, He knew which blessed angel to take.
I regret not giving my Sweetness a final kiss. One day our time together will be endless. Happy 1st birthday. Loving you Always...Mommie, Grandma, and Granddad

September 6, 1997
Mommie thought you'd be an AKA with me; you're initiated into a grander sorority! My line name is Buried Treasure—You are now my Buried Treasure. Missing you on your first anniversary.
Love eternally, Mommie.

March 31, 1998
Time's not measured by the years you live, but by the deeds you do and the joy you give.
What does it matter how long we may live, as long as we live we unselfishly give.

Haven's your sister. Like you, in a safe and secure place. You two share much, a middle name and my love. Happy 2nd birthday.
Love eternally, Mommie & Haven

September 6, 1998
You have helped us to learn that prayer pushes light and hope into the dark corners of our lives. Thank you.
Love eternally, Mommie & Haven

March 31, 1999
We don't question God about our blessings, so we should not question Him about our troubles.
Thank you for a great lesson.
Love eternally, Mommie & Haven

September 6, 1999
Each day I love you more...today more than yesterday...and less than tomorrow.
Love eternally, Mommie & Haven

March 31, 2000
Our life of service to the Lord bears fruit long after we are gone.
So even if our life's cut short, our work for Christ will carry on.
Happy 4th birthday.
Love Mommie & Haven

September 6, 2000
God is good, all the time and all the time, God is good.
Missing you today and forever.
Love eternally, Mommie & Haven

March 31, 2001
The things we overcome in life really become our strengths. Missing you today and forever.
Happy 5th birthday.
Love eternally, Mommie & Haven

September 6, 2001
"If you worry, why pray; if you pray, why worry?"

The joy of having you is greater than the pain of losing you. Thanks for faith and strength lessons.
Mommie & Haven

March 31, 2002
You have helped us to understand that if we have a problem that man can solve, we really do not have a problem. Happy 6th Easter birthday, Punkin'.
Mommie & Haven

September 6, 2002
When we die, we leave behind all we have and take with us all we are. Part of me went with you. Happy 6th anniversary, Punkin'.
Mommie, Haven, & October sibling

March 31, 2003
While the child was alive, I fasted and wept: for I said, Who can tell whether God will be gracious to me, that the child may live? I shall go to him, but he shall not return to me.
Mommie, Haven & Christian

September 6, 2003
Dear Angel, ever at my side, how lovely you must be. To leave your home in Heaven to guard a soul like me.
Love eternally, Mommie, Haven, and Christian

March 31, 2004
While the child was alive, I fasted and wept: for I said, Who can tell whether God will be gracious to me, that the child may live? I shall go to him, but he shall not return to me.
Mommie , Haven & Christian

September 6, 2004
Because I could not stop for death, He kindly stopped for me. The carriage held but just ourselves – and immortality. Miss you!
Love, Mommie, Haven and Christian

March 31, 2005
If God came from Heaven and let me choose the greatest gift it would be you. To me you are still special, God must have thought so, too.

Love, Mommie, Haven and Christian

September 6, 2005
It's reasons only God can give to put my mind at rest, but I know it's true – He only takes the best. Love on your 9th anniversary.
Mommie, Haven and Christian

March 31, 2006
Kayla,
You were taken much too quickly, so early, so small, but I know you belong in Gods arms after all. I can't ever pick you up or hold you very tight. And I'll never cuddle you when you cry out for me at night. Now you are God's little angel who will watch your siblings grow to be wonderful people and whose love they will always know. You'll always be a part of me, within my heart you'll stay. It's you I'm always thinking of each night and every day. I wish I only had the chance to see you just once more to tell you, Kayla, I love you and kiss you many times like I had before. Happy 10th Birthday
Mommie, Haven & Christian

September 6, 2006
They who are near me do not know that you are nearer to me than they are...
Those who speak to me do not know that my heart is full with your unspoken words...
Those who crowd my path do not know that I am walking alone with you...
They who love me do not know that their love brings you to my heart...
It's been 10 years since you left!
Love eternally, Mommie, Haven & Christian

m
ctor, PICU
nc.org

. MD

.org

ir, MD

ic.org

arts, MD

imc.org

lonim, MD
irector
nc.org

Dear Ms. Anthony,

Thank you so much for your thoughtfulness. It is so nice to be appreciated. I do remember you and Kayla and I am thankful that you and your family are getting along after such an ordeal.

I will share your thoughts with the whole Intensive Care Unit staff. Let me assure you your donation will be put to very good use.

Sincerely,

Murray M. Pollack, MD
Director, Critical Care Medicine
Executive Director, Center for Hospital-Based Specialties

Dear Mrs. Anthony:

On behalf of Children's National Medical Center, it is my pleasure to acknowledge your gift of $765.00 to Critical Care Medicine in memory of your daughter. We deeply appreciate your concern for the well being of our young patients.

It is through the generosity of individuals like you that Children's is able to take giant steps towards our goal to be the preeminent pediatric healthcare provider regionally, nationally and internationally. With your help, Children's is able to perform thousands of life-saving procedures each year on infants, children and adolescents.

For 130 years our mission has been to provide the highest quality of care to all the children who come to us, regardless of their ability to pay. We are able to fulfill this mission because of contributions from donors like you. Thank you for making a difference in the lives of children.

Sincerely,

Danielle Weaver
Major Gifts Officer

Footprints on the Heart
by Flavia Weedn

Some people come into our lives and quickly go.
Some people move our souls to dance.
They awaken us to new understanding
with the passing whisper of their wisdom.

Some people make the sky more beautiful to gaze upon.
They stay in our lives for awhile,
leave footprints on our hearts
And we are never, ever the same.

SUPPORTING THOSE WHO HAVE LOST A CHILD

"Thou wilt keep him in perfect peace, whose mind is stayed on thee: because he trusteth in thee." ~Isaiah 26:3

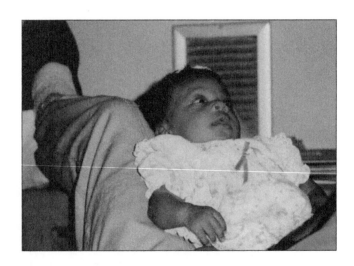

Not surprisingly, it often takes longer for parents to move through the grieving process of having lost their child than those who have lost other loved ones. The overwhelming sense of loss is often magnified if the loss was sudden as there is little time to "prepare" and grieve the impending–yet completely unexpected–loss. There is no time period in which parents will be "over" the loss. It has taken me quite a number of years to accept that the blessings I have received since the death of my beloved daughter far outweigh the nearly insurmountable loss experienced. Part of my accepting the reality of my blessings came after I recognized that the acceptance of my blessings does not diminish the impact of my loss and is in no way disrespectful to my daughter or her memory. I can continue to love her eternally while being eternally grateful for positive occurrences since she died. Perhaps I am better able to appreciate what I have received due to the fact that I realize just how quickly it can all be taken away from me.

> *Losing a child is like an amputation, one moment an important piece of you is there and then suddenly, it's gone.*

Beware of Offensive Behavior

There are those who certainly mean well, but sadly, they are perhaps self-centered, misinformed, or simply ignorant. Some have said things to me that may have been well intended yet had an unintended impact as their words were essentially hurtful and unappreciated. Examples of what was said to me directly:

1. *"You will have other children."* When Kayla first died, I was only focused on her in the present and not children I might have in the future. The only thing I wanted was for her to be the unaffected child to whom I had given birth. After hearing that one too many times, I began to respond, *"If my husband had died, you would not suggest that I get married again."* I was not looking to "replace" my child, but to attempt to handle—in the best way I could fathom—what no parent should ever have to experience.
2. A perceptive stranger at the post office read my face and said, *"It's not that bad."* I replied, *"My child died."* End of interaction.
3. *"I know how you feel."* No you do not. The loss of a parent or sibling cannot be equated to the loss of a child. Even if you have lost a child, no one knows how I feel as the only one who has also lost that particular child is the other parent. Even with the other parent, all of our interactions are different and all of us experience grief differently. No one can

really "understand" how another feels—not even the other parent—because the circumstances are different, the relationships are different, and we as individuals are different.

4. X lost their child at the age of X which makes it harder for them. It is so hard for me to fathom how that is in any way comforting. Although I lost my child at five months, six days, and twelve hours old, my guess is that nearly every parent feels that they have it "worse"—especially while their emotions remain raw.

5. My loss was not only unexpected because Kayla was in an accident, but having your child predecease you is not something anyone ever anticipates in life. Having limited photos and memories and unfulfilled dreams for the future are difficult when a child dies so young. When any of us are in the midst of a very difficult situation, we often feel "alone" and that we are the only one to experience such a tragedy. We need to allow bereaved parents whatever amount of time they need to accept their circumstances as they are and not try to feel that your loss or another's loss "trumps" what that person is processing. We need to be supportive and encouraging of one another, in my opinion, and not think that we are indeed "the most miserable" as we may in reality minimize or dismiss the pain of the one we are attempting to help.

6. *"It could have been worse."* Although that is most likely always true, it is by no means consoling. Considering an analogy to demonstrate the point, if a mugger only put out one of your eyes instead of both, there is little consolation for someone to point out to you that you "only" lost one eye—especially when the loss is first experienced. You may come to the point of appreciating what remains, but it must be the person who has experienced the loss to grow to that conclusion independently and in their own time.

7. *"Your child is in a better place."* As Christians, many of us do indeed believe this to be true and I am one to believe that when we die, our spirit indeed goes directly to Heaven. However, when you have lost a child—especially

unexpectedly—it often takes time to see that your child has been relieved of the pain and suffering of this world. Initially, I was "selfishly" focused on myself and the acute pain that I was experiencing instead of reflecting on the fact that my child would not suffer a life tethered to tubes for feeding. With the mugger analogy, the person who lost one eye may feel that they can now appreciate and "see" life and their blessings differently, but that is most likely not automatic. In grieving, the loss is permanent and the pain is often continually severe for many years. Still, I find myself overwhelmed with a rush of grief for no obvious reason, but those events are, thankfully, less frequent and less intense.

For Outsiders

1. Express sympathy and feel free to express that you do not know what to say. In reality, that can be comforting. Truthfully, bereaved parents do not know what we need or want to hear as nothing said will really make the situation "better." Saying, *"I don't know what to say, but I want you to know that I am so sorry and I wish I could do more. We are praying for you and thinking of you,"* is just fine. It is truthful, honest, direct, and does no harm. Actually, it may even do some good because the bereaved parent is not forced to "take care of" the speaker. We are not made to feel that our child can be easily replaced by another and we feel we are able to connect with the caring individual. There are no words or emotions created to make the devastating situation any less painful so by all means, do not say or do something that will further burden the family emotionally.

2. Anticipate, with patience, inappropriate behavior and emotions. When a person acts inappropriately because of stress, it does little, if any, good to increase the stress by attacking the stressed out individual and making them feel ostracized. They and their feelings are in need of care and not someone else's.

3. Often, especially if the financial strain has been severe and funds are being collected, it is wise to provide support and

help in managing donated funds. We are not able to think clearly and rationally, but can greatly benefit from having others handle some of the day-to-day challenges we do not have the emotional resources to consider early on. Even offering to assist with managing household finances relieves pressure so that we do not later have to deal having fallen behind on bills.

4. Do not ignore all references to the dead child as the child is dead, not erased. Our child continues to be important to us although we do not know how others will take our ongoing references to our child. Sometimes, others feel uncomfortable and have us to feel we are pathological, "stuck," creating a "shrine" as they are the ones that want to put the death of our child behind them. I really like how the late Elizabeth Edwards, whose sixteen-year-old son Wade died in a car accident, verbalized her loss when she said, *"I have had to learn how to parent a memory."* Allowing a grieving family to discuss their child often helps a great deal. We know that others realize our child continues to be important to us and is on our mind daily. Once, I asked someone if they were going to call a close friend on her deceased child's birthday. This person relied, *"I don't want to remind her of the birthday."* My response, *"She remembers."*

5. October happens to be National Pregnancy and Infant Loss Month. Consider reaching out to families then, during the child's birthday and anniversary of the child's death, during holidays, or just because. These occasions are often quite difficult for bereaved parents. Many do not want to "burden" others with their sadness which can actually be quite isolating. We often do not have the strength to ask for what we need and thus need others to consider what it is that they are able to provide.

6. At the family members' own pace, allow them to participate in social activities. It is generally best to continue family members' involvement in previously held positions. We need to be supported in our weakness rather than being released from everything. When a child dies, we need

increased supports instead of having others to alienate us. It is important for those who lose children to move forward and not give in to despair. Being involved in life, social activities, and church helps the healing process as long as well wishers do not overwhelm the grieving parent. Immediately after Kayla died, I was asked to be involved in, quite frankly, too many church activities. As much as I appreciated being remembered, I felt that I was not able to say, *"No"* to the requests because perhaps I was saying *"No"* to something God wanted me to do. Eventually, I gained the strength not to continually over commit myself, but rather engage in the activities that were most meaningful, and guilt-free, to me.

7. Finally, realize that the need for patience and resolving grief are both long-term processes with no time limit. If you are not able to help, at least do not try to rush the person to overcome their grief in a predetermined period because you are uncomfortable. Again, we all grieve differently and one bereaved parent cannot tell another bereaved parent how long it will "take" to resolve the loss. The pain will not be over in a week or even several months. The recovery may not be stable until years later with the bereaved parents cycling through stages previously encountered. The most common results of attempting to rush recovery are increased stress and unintentionally forcing the bereaved parent to be stuck in one of the stages of grief (usually denial). Rushing grief is often the most harmful thing someone can do to a grieving parent. It is usually done because those around us do not know how to handle our emotional upsets. Others may choose to rush another's grief to make themselves feel better rather than to help the bereaved parent to feel better.

For Bereaved Family Members

No matter how much you may want the contrary to be true, nothing cures the pain of losing a child. There are some things, however, that may actually help you to lessen the intense suffering of those you care about to some degree.

1. Many support groups exist and can be extremely helpful. Being with those who have been through the pain and loss of a child can often make all the difference in the world. Help the bereaved parent to find a group that suits them. I attended a group that I did not feel was a good fit for me as I was not able to share experiences I had had with my child throughout the years. A more appropriate group for me was one which consisted of parents who had also lost infants. We could relate to grieving for the future that was not to be as well as the grief of having limited memories.

2. Give unlimited grace to the bereaved family as dealing with the loss is debilitating and often a lifelong process.

3. Continually move forward because if you stop, everything stops with you. In addition to having had a child to die, you still have living family and friends who love and care tremendously about you. If you have surviving children, regardless of their age, remember that they, too, are grieving and are in need of support as well. If you are not able to provide what your surviving children need physically or emotionally, elicit the help of others so that you do not compound your stress by becoming a neglectful parent. Although it may seem impossible, the sooner you return to some semblance of work (even at reduced hours), the sooner your mind will focus on healing. Prior to Kayla's death, my work hours were 7:00 a.m. until 3:00 p.m. I returned to work about three weeks following her death as I had very little leave since I had been granted three months' maternity leave. I chose to work from 6:00 a.m. until 12:00 noon. This was a great arrangement since I was not able to sleep plus I was having minor panic attacks and groups were extremely difficult for me.

4. Reduce stress as much as possible. Following the death of your child, it is certainly a time to prioritize and let things go that do not require your immediate attention. Keep a journal, pray, get mild aerobic exercise, and seek support whether it is via family and friends or a support group.

5. Find places to express your rage, fear, pain, hurt, rejection, and confusion. You will certainly have all of these emotions – and

perhaps others—with great intensity. It will be difficult to express them in an "appropriate" way and thus it is best to find a safe, private place to channel your emotions without the judgment and concern of others. Family members often require these same outlets as we will attempt to protect those we love to the best of our ability which can mean that we do not take needed time for ourselves.

6. Guard against becoming bitter. It is extremely hard for others to believe that I was not angry at God for taking Kayla from me. I may be the exception, but honestly, I was never angry at God or the babysitter. I realize just how accurate that was because I was definitely angry with Him about another situation that occurred later. While Kayla was still hospitalized, I told the babysitter, *"We are vehicles by which the Lord's will is done."* I always knew that children were gifts from God and that we must cherish them for whatever length of time we are blessed to be connected to one another physically. I, of course, thought that I would be the one to leave this earth first, however.

7. Turn toward those you love rather than away because this is imperative if relationships are to survive significant loss. If you turn toward each other rather than inward when under stress, you are likely to change the odds of severing the relationship from nearly 100% against you to nearly 100% in your favor by controlling this one factor. This reality is a matter of personal choice and control and we need both during a time when choice and control has been removed.

The death of a child is a terrible loss that destroys many families. Often, the fate of a family or its members hangs by a thread. By providing love and understanding without hypocrisy or guilt and with God's grace and mercy, families can be supported in their pain and aided on the path to healing.

Information Regarding Infant Death

Unintentional deaths from suffocation and strangulation account for about one-fifth of all non-transport related infant and child fatalities in the United States. In the late 1950s, some preventive countermeasures were introduced to reduce the number of deaths resulting from refrigerator or freezer entrapment. A few years later, countermeasures were introduced to prevent deaths resulting from suffocation by plastic bags, inhumation, and mechanical strangulation from wedging in infant cribs. There appears to have been a significant decline in infant deaths from the above-mentioned methods with the exception of death from mechanical strangulation in cribs. Many of these deaths can often be prevented if parents and caregivers watch their children more closely and take steps to improve safety in the home, especially the sleeping areas.

Background

There are approximately 21 million children under age 6 in this country and nearly three-quarters are placed in non-parental child care during some portion of the day. About one-third of these children are in center-based care, including day care centers, Head Start programs, and nursery schools. Those remaining are in non-center-based care, including family child care, in-home child care, and care by a relative.

To reduce the chances of suffocation:

Child suffocation deaths result when the child is unable to breathe and there may be no clinical findings when an autopsy is conducted. This is the fourth leading type of accidental death for all children, following motor vehicle crashes, fires, and drowning. It is only through a comprehensive scene investigation that unintentional suffocation can be distinguished from SIDS or intentional suffocations and may still be reported as "undetermined." Most unintentional suffocations are caused by:

<u>Overlay</u>:

a person who is sleeping with a child rolls onto the child and unintentionally smothers the child. The majority of infants suffocated die in this way. Infants sleeping in adult beds are 20 times more likely to suffocate than infants who sleep alone in cribs. If the caregiver is obese, overly fatigued, or under the influence of alcohol or drugs, even over-the-counter and prescription drugs, the incidence of suffocation is significantly increased. Some proponents of bed sharing argue that it promotes breastfeeding. I am guilty of that. However, the benefits received from bed sharing can be derived from the practice of having the infant sleep on a separate, firm surface while in the same room with the mother.

Positional asphyxia:

a child's face becomes trapped in soft bedding or is wedged in a small space such as between a mattress and a wall or between couch cushions.

Covering of face or chest:

an object covers a child's face or compresses the chest, such as plastic bags, heavy blankets, or furniture.

Choking:

a child chokes on an object such as a piece of food or small toy. For choking and strangulation deaths, toddlers and preschoolers are at highest risk due to the fact that they are active, become entangled in cords, and gain access to small objects. Food and uninflated balloons remain the number one and two choking hazards, respectively, again usually for toddlers.

Confinement:

a child is trapped in an airtight place such as an unused refrigerator, toy chest, or trunk of a car.

Strangulation:

a rope, cords, hands, or other objects strangle a child. In the case of Kayla, it was a television tray. Product safety improvements have decreased the number of strangulations due to the scrutiny and recalls on toys with choking hazards, removal of draws rings from children's clothing, and safety cord hangers for window blinds.

High quality of supervision is always the best prevention. There are, however, additional preventive measures that can be taken:

At Bedtime
1. Place babies to sleep on their backs on a firm, flat mattress.
2. Do not use pillows or heavy comforters in the crib.
3. Make sure the crib mattress is big enough for the crib. The space between the crib slats and the mattress should be smaller than the width of two adult fingers.
4. Never let the baby sleep in bed with you. A tremendously high number of babies have died when their breathing was blocked by pillows, bedding, and even their parents. More than three-quarters of infant deaths of children younger than three months old occurred when they were placed in an adult bed, including water beds and daybeds. Infants and children can suffocate or strangle when they become entrapped between the mattress and the wall, bed frame, headboard, footboard, bed railings, or adjacent furniture. Mothers who breastfeed should be alerted to this hazard and should be encouraged to return the baby to the crib after breastfeeding.
5. Bed rails, which are portable railings that can be installed on toddler and adult beds to keep toddlers from falling out of beds, also account for infant deaths.

Around the House
1. Keep plastic shopping, garbage, and dry cleaning bags away from babies and children. Never use a plastic shipping bag or other plastic film as a mattress cover.
2. Choose a toy chest without a lid. If the toy chest has a lid, make sure it has a safety latch that stays open in any position. Ensure there are holes in the back and/or bottom of the chest to allow air flow in case your child gets stuck inside.

3. Lock your car, including the trunk, when it is not in use because many children have died after climbing into car trunks and becoming trapped. Always supervise children around cars and keep keys away from them. Children can also manage to open car trunks themselves, with or without keys. While hyperthermia (becoming too hot) is the most frequent cause of death, asphyxia (suffocation) is also a contributing factor in many of these deaths.

To reduce the chances of strangulation:
In the Crib
1. Check with the U.S. Consumer Product Safety Commission before buying a new or second-hand crib to make sure it has not been recalled. More babies die annually in incidents involving cribs than with any other piece of nursery equipment. The majority of these are older, used cribs.
2. Make sure the slats on your crib are no more than 2 3/8 inches apart or babies can slide through the slats and strangle when their heads get stuck. Babies can suffocate or strangle when they become trapped between broken crib parts or between parts of an older crib with an unsafe design.
3. Do not use a crib with cut outs in the end panels or with corner posts more than 1/16 inch higher than the end panels. Strangulation can occur if a baby's clothing gets caught on a high corner post or if a baby's head gets caught in a cut out.
4. Remove your baby's bib before bedtime or nap time.
5. Remove mobiles and crib gyms as soon as your baby is five months old or can push up on their hands and knees.

Around the House
1. Pull drapery and mini blind cords out of children's reach and away from cribs. If the cords have a loop, cut the loop and attach separate tassels to avoid strangulation. For additional safety, cribs should not be placed near windows.
2. If your child has a bunk bed, check the guard rails on the top bunk. There should be only a very small space between the

rail and the mattress or bed frame so the child's body cannot slide through.

3. Do not let your child lie in or play with a hammock that does not have spreader bars (wooden strips at the ends of the hammock that stop the netting from bunching up). Mini hammocks, often used to store toys and stuffed animals, are also a hazard because the child can get entangled in them.

4. Remove hood cords and drawstrings from the child's clothing. These cords can become entangled in playground equipment, fences, or furniture causing strangulation.

5. Remove loose ribbons or strings on toys and stuffed animals. Never use a string or ribbon to tie a pacifier or toy to your baby.

6. Safety gates can prevent a wide range of injuries, especially falls down stairs.

Prevention

1. Education at childbirth classes and in hospitals are offered to expectant and new parents on safe infant sleep environments.

2. Hospital assessments by nurses with parents to assess babies' sleep environments is often available.

3. Culturally competent public education campaigns and coordination with the "Back to Sleep" campaign is worth exploring.

4. There are crib distribution programs for needy families.

5. Education to professionals on risks of infant suffocation is something to seriously consider and it is often free.

6. Monitor continued product safety recalls on choking and strangulation hazards.

7. Licensing requirements for daycare providers on safe sleep environments and infant sleep positions should be frequently assessed and updated.

Young children can be seriously hurt from falls on playgrounds.

1. For children under age six, playground-related injuries account for more visits to U.S. hospital emergency rooms

than any other child care-related injury and some are fatal injuries. Most injuries occur when a child falls from the equipment onto the ground and sustains fractures.

2. To help protect children from serious injuries, especially head injuries, safe playground surfacing should have at least 12 inches of wood chips, mulch, sand, pea gravel, or rubber or rubber-like materials. The surfacing should be properly maintained so that dirt, grass, glass, bricks, and asphalt are removed.

My Beloved
by Ruth Scott

The pearly gates are open wide,
To let an angel come inside.
No more tears no more pain,
Just sweet peace forever to reign.
You've done your work here on earth,
None but God knows your heavenly worth.
The Master's voice you did obey,
His praise you sang both night and day,
Though friends and family weep for you,
We understand our heavenly Father needed you.
The time we shared was just a loan,
For now He's called you to your heavenly home.
Our hearts may be heavy and our tears may fall,
We're not to question for Christ knows all.

The Weaver
author unknown

My life is but a weaving between my Lord and me,
I cannot choose the colors He worketh steadily.

Oftimes He weaveth sorrow, and I in foolish pride
Forget He sees the upper, and I, the underside.

Not till the loom is silent and the shuttles cease to fly
Shall God unroll the canvas and explain the reason why.

The dark threads are as needful in the Weaver's skillful hand
As the threads of gold and silver in the pattern He has planned.

THE WASHINGTON POST

"When suffering comes, we yearn for some sign from God, forgetting we just had one." ~Mignon McLaughlin

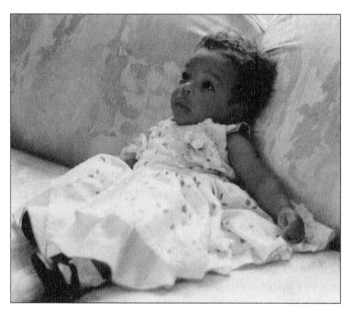

An Open Letter to Bereaved Parents
by Ann Landers

I won't say, "I know how you feel" — because I don't. I've lost parents, grandparents, aunts, uncles and friends, but I've never lost a child. So how can I say I know how you feel?

I won't say, "You'll get over it" — because you never will. Life will, however, have to go on. The washing, cooking, cleaning, the common routine. The chores will take your mind off your loved one, but the hurt will still be there.

I won't say, "Your other children will be a comfort to you" — because they may not be. Many mothers I've talked to say that after they have lost a child, they easily lose their temper with their remaining children. Some even feel resentful that they're alive and healthy, when the other child is not.

I won't say, "Never mind, you're young enough to have another baby" — because that won't help. A new baby cannot replace the one you've lost. A new baby will fill your hours, keep you busy, give you sleepless nights, but it will never replace the one you've lost.

You may hear all these platitudes from your friends and relatives. They think they are helping. They don't know what else to say. You will find out who your true friends are at this time. Many will avoid you because they can't face you. Others will talk about the weather, the holidays and the school concert but never about your child. Never about how you are coping. So what will I say?

I will say, *"I'm here. I care. Anytime. Anywhere."* I'll cry with you if need be. I'll talk about your loved one. We'll laugh about the good memories. I won't mind how long you grieve. I won't tell you to pull yourself together.

No, I don't know how you feel — but with sharing, perhaps I will learn a little of what you are going through. And maybe you will feel comfortable with me and find your burden eased. Try me.

"Family Almanac"
by Marguerite Kelly
May 9, 2003

I've written the Family Almanac for 25 years, not because I'm so wise, but because I'm so interested in the questions I get.

Parents have the most exhilarating, amusing, creative job in the world, and the most exhausting, demanding, relentless one, too. Somehow they are expected to do their best, day after day, even when they're scrambling to pay the rent or hold their marriage together or work for a wretched boss.

I've answered questions on everything from addictions to bedwetting; day care to college; self-confidence to sex, but this time I'm the one with the problem and I don't know how to solve it.

Our only son, Mike – an embedded journalist in Iraq – was rushing towards Baghdad Airport on April 3rd when his Humvee was ambushed, causing it to flip upside down and fall into a canal. Death was quick, but grief, I find, keeps going on and on and on and it affects me in strange ways.

I feel no denial. No anger. No bargaining. No depression. And this makes me wonder if I'll ever get to peace and acceptance. These five classic stages of grief, cited so authoritatively by Elizabeth Kubler-Ross, aren't working for me.

Instead my grief is amorphous, deceitful, unpredictable. Sometimes it hides behind distractions; sometimes it covers my spirits like the pall on Mike's coffin, and sometimes it knocks me flat, particularly when I think of Mike's beloved wife, Max, and their little boys, Tom, 7, and Jack, 3, who must live their lives without him.

I tell myself to get grief counseling or to go to the excellent, free support meetings of The Compassionate Friends, for parents who have lost a child at any age; to see sad movies so I can get rid of my tears; to read The Lively Shadow by Donald M. Murray, a wonderfully understated, cathartic book about the death of his grown daughter, and, of course, I tell myself to pray, but mostly I remember my son as he really was. Not perfect, of course, but he was mine and he suited us so well.

Mike's political column could be fierce and it infuriated some readers, but he was a sunny, funny fellow who made fun of himself, easily and often. That boy could make a dog laugh.

A humble man, an honest man – a moralist, really – he was always true to himself. Although sometimes given to hyperbole, he said what he meant, whether anyone liked it or not, and he never ran away from a bully, either on the playground as a child or on the battlefield as a man.

He challenged his bosses, too, and he did it as freely and as often as he challenged popular opinion, but he also cosseted and encouraged the young people he worked with, because he knew they would only love to write when they could do it well.

It was his own love of writing, and not the money or the glory it brought him, that made Mike change jobs every 2-3 years. As soon as he mastered the skills he needed to work for a particular TV show or newspaper or magazine, he wanted to move on. There was always more to learn.

As much as Mike loved to write, to accomplish, and to think, he loved his family much more and he spent almost all his free time with them.

Mike threw himself into life and paid total, intense attention to the things that were important to him. He cooked splendid dinners for his wife; kayaked with his boys, told them wacky stories at night, and had them help him make small repairs around the house: the Three-Man Fixing Company. He also dug in his garden with delight; ironed his own shirts (badly); painted his beach house (beautifully); called his sisters, his father, and me whenever he could; and read history, took long walks, and occasionally went on retreats to meditate and pray.

Clothes were not among his priorities and neither were the necessities of modern life. He bought his ties at thrift shops, wore frayed shirts and holey sweaters, and lost his ATM card, his cell phone, his credit cards, and his driver's license over and over again, but he always made time for the people he liked and especially the people he loved. Lost memories, he knew, could not be replaced.

But now it's my son who can't be replaced and he mattered so much to me. There is no right time to lose a child.

December 3, 2004

Question:

My daughter died suddenly, a month ago, leaving her husband, her 12-year-old son, and me to mourn.

She was very close to her son and they had a wonderful relationship, but he hasn't spoken of his mother's death since then. He did cry a little at her funeral and he has read many cards sent to him, but that's all.

Now he is back at school and pursuing all the activities he was involved in before she died, but he still hasn't talked about his mother.

Is there anything I can do to help him? I see him each day, as I have for years, and we have always been very close. Is it possible that he may need professional help? Please tell me what is happening.

Answer:
Therapy would probably help any child who has lost a parent, but your grandson may not be able to open up to a grief counselor for another few months. Children need time to adjust to the reality of death.

Even when your grandson is ready for one-on-one counseling or for a support group made up of other grieving children, he may not want to go at first. Memories are so precious—and so elusive—that children often hate to share them with anyone.

In the meantime—and for all time—your grandson needs extra support from all the amateur helpers in his world: his buddies, his teacher, his minister, his daddy—and especially his grandma.

Your son-in-law may be able to get his boy to talk about his mother—if he's not too grief-stricken or too inhibited—but you may be able to draw him out better, because you see him so often and you are so close to him. Just don't expect him to initiate the conversation; his grief is too raw for that.

Instead, ask him to help you organize all those snapshots and mementos and letters you've saved from his mom's childhood and even pay him for doing it. By turning this work into a job, you will be letting him stay in his cocoon a little longer, even as you unravel it by telling him about his mother when she was a child.

These stories will give you the chance to talk about your daughter and give him stories to tell his children about their grandmother one day. As the Jewish prayer lovingly says,

"So long as we live, they too shall live,

for they are now a part of us as
we remember them."

Bit by bit your grandson will talk about his own memories, too, and when he does, you should talk about your feelings so he will begin to talk about his. When he does, you'll know that both of you are ready for a little grief counseling.

The Compassionate Friends, a free support group for parents who have lost a child of any age, for any reason, would be a good one for you and it has chapters all over the world. The unfortunate participants of this 'been there, done that' group can probably steer you to the best therapists or support groups for your grandson and your son-in-law as well. If he will go, too, the three of you can work through your grief at about the same pace which is important. If your timing is out of whack, your relationships may become out of whack, too, and then professional help will be a must.

Whether your family gets help or not, you should continue the customs and rituals that were dear to your daughter and you should also commemorate her life in little ways: a sprig of rosemary—for remembrance—on the kitchen table; a small, but regular contribution to a charity in her name, and Sunday school for your grandson, so he can say special prayers for his mother.

You'll also want to ask him and his dad to join you on December 12, when parents all over the world will light candles in memory of the children they've lost. This custom, sponsored by The Compassionate Friends, begins at 7:00 p.m., local time, and lasts an hour, so that there will be 'a 24-hour wave of light' as the time changes around the globe.

And to understand the way grief affects the young, read Helen Fitzgerald's classic book, <u>The Grieving Child</u>. You should find it extremely helpful.

March 25, 2005

Question:

The first anniversary of the birth and death of our grandson is approaching and my daughter and son-in-law don't know how to mark it.

He was a sweet boy, perfect in all ways, but he suffered an accident at birth and lived for only one day.

Now the parents are wondering how to commemorate his short life. There was no service at that time, though their friends arranged a gathering at a nearby park. We joined in a circle, singing, while a candle was lit. My grandsons, then 4 and 6, participated, along with their pals.

This year the parents want to plan something memorable with the family and are looking for suggestions. So far, they plan a small dedication ceremony at their new home, which is along a small river, and to place a natural-style rock, etched with his name, near the water. They say they will observe this day every year.

Answer:

First of all, congratulate your daughter and son-in-law for dealing with their grief in such a healthy way.

The death of a child who lived, however briefly, is as much a tragedy as any other death and it should not be ignored.

If parents hide their sorrow, they will withdraw or get testy or dive into their work or run away from their marriage, as if any of those things could make their pain go away. It's much better for them to celebrate their child's life and to talk about their loss freely and whenever they want.

Having a ceremony in the park to mark his death was appropriate and so is a family event to celebrate his life. If the parents are religious, your daughter could ask a minister to bless the site when it's dedicated and to talk about the baby as their 'guardian angel', as some families do. Or the parents could simply talk about the child and what he meant to them and his big brothers could each read a letter they had written to him or show a picture they painted for him or a dance they made up for him.

Your daughter could also bake a cake for this occasion, so everyone could sing 'Happy Birthday' and blow out a candle – the favorite tradition with some parents. Another family celebrates their child's birthday with a 5-minute ceremony, where they sign a birthday card, tie it to a balloon, make a silent wish, and let the balloon float away. According to this family, heaven is very high and to the left.

Your daughter can even take a card and a balloon with her if she has to be away on her son's birthday, because she can go through this ritual wherever she is.

You might also suggest that she pick up a small stone from the riverbank, etch it with the baby's name, and keep it on a table in the house, so she can put it on the dinner table for a special occasion or simply touch it as she goes by.

Neither she nor her husband should feel bound to follow this or any custom however. What is right for one family can be wrong for another.

They also shouldn't follow any tradition past its natural time. Although your other grandsons may almost forget their little brother's existence 10 years from now, his parents never will. The grief they feel now will lessen however, and so will their need to express it.

Some parents may tell you that the observance of these traditions could upset the surviving siblings, but that's unlikely.

Children need to realize that life is a cycle of birth and death and as necessary as sunshine and rain. Once they know that, they will be able to accept any death better, no matter how much they loved the person who died.

To help the boys accept this reality, you might give them a book called <u>After You Lose Someone You Love</u> written by three children, Amy, Allie, and David Dennison. The text is drawn from the dairies they kept for two years after their father died.

You might also give your daughter a CD written by country music star George Canyon called <u>One Good Friend</u>, because it includes his recording of "My Name." This song is about a miscarriage – the most ignored, and perhaps the most poignant death of all – and one that may come closest to your daughter's experience. It may help her get through her second year of grief, which can be even more painful than the first.

THE WASHINGTON POST

Family Almanac

A Problem With No Solution: The Death of a Beloved Child

By MARGUERITE KELLY
Special to The Washington Post

I've written the Family Almanac for 25 years, not because I'm so wise but because I'm so interested in the questions I get.

Parents have the most exhilarating, arousing, creative job in the world, and the most exhausting, demanding, relentless one, too. Somehow they are expected to do their best, day after day, even when they're scrambling to pay the rent or hold their marriage together or work for a wretched boss.

I've answered questions on everything from addictions to bed-wetting, day care to college, self-confidence to sex, but this time I'm the one with the problem and I don't know how to solve it.

Our only son, Mike—an embedded journalist in Iraq—was rushing toward Baghdad Airport on April 3 when his Humvee was ambushed, causing it to flip upside down and fall into a canal. Death was quick, but grief, I find, keeps going on and on and on and it affects me in strange ways.

I feel no denial. No anger. No bargaining. No depression. And this makes me wonder if I'll ever get to peace and acceptance. These five classic stages of grief, cited so authoritatively by Elisabeth Kubler-Ross, aren't working for me.

Instead my grief is amorphous, deceitful, unpredictable. Sometimes it hides behind distractions; sometimes it covers my spirits like the pall on Mike's coffin, and sometimes it knocks me flat, particularly when I think of Mike's beloved wife, Max, and their little boys, Tom, 7, and Jack, 3, who must live their lives without him.

I tell myself to get grief counseling or to go to the excellent, free support meetings of the Compassionate Friends, for parents who have lost a child at any age; to see sad movies so I can get rid of my tears; to read "The Lively Shadow" by Donald M. Murray, a wonderfully understated, cathartic book about the death of his grown daughter; and, of course, I tell myself to pray. But mostly I remember my son as he really was. Not perfect, of course, but he was mine and he suited us so well.

Mike's political column could be fierce and it infuriated some readers, but he was a sunny, funny fellow who made fun of himself, easily

and often. That boy could make a dog laugh.

A humble man, an honest man—a moralist, really—he was always true to himself. Although he sometimes given to hyperbole, he said what he meant, whether anyone liked it or not, and he never ran away from a bully, either on the playground as a child or on the battlefield as a man.

He challenged his bosses, too, and he did it as freely and as often as he challenged popular opinion, but he also cosseted and encouraged the young people he worked with, because he knew they would only love to write when they could do it well.

It was his own love of writing, and not the money or the glory it brought him, that made Mike change jobs every two to three years. As soon as he mastered the skills he needed to work for a particular TV show or newspaper or magazine, he wanted ed to move on. There was always more to learn.

As much as Mike loved to write, to accomplish and to think, he loved his family much more and he spent almost all of his free time with them.

Mike threw himself into life and paid total, intense attention to the things that were important to him. He cooked splendid dinners for his wife; kayaked with his boys, told them wacky stories at night and had them help him make small repairs around the house; the Three-Man Fixing Company. He also dug in his garden with delight; ironed his own shirts (badly); painted his beach house (beautifully); called his sisters, his father and me whenever he could; and read history, took long walks and occasionally went on retreats to meditate and pray.

Clothes were not among his priorities, and neither were the necessities of modern life. He bought his ties at thrift shops, wore frayed shirts and holey sweaters and lost his ATM card, his cell phone, his credit cards and his driver's license over and over again, but he always made time for the people he liked and especially the people he loved. Lost memories, he knew, could not be replaced.

But now it's my son who can't be replaced, and he mattered so much to me. There is no right time to lose a child.

Journalist Michael Kelly was killed in Iraq when his ambushed Humvee flipped over.

Questions? Send them to advice@margueritekelly.com or to Box 15310, Washington D.C. 20003.

You're Still with Me
author unknown

Though you are gone
I know you are still with me
In the simple things
I used to never see.

One day while walking
I chanced to see
A butterfly
Seeming to follow me.

In the yard one day
A little bluebird up in a tree
Singing its song
To no one, but me.

Then early one morning
Right after the sunrise
On a rosebush where no roses ever grew
Was a beautiful rose, much to my surprise.

All these things happened for a reason
Just for me to see
It's just your way of showing
You are still with me.

A NEW UNDERSTANDING

"Trials are part of life just like humps on the road."
~Nala Aled Zurc

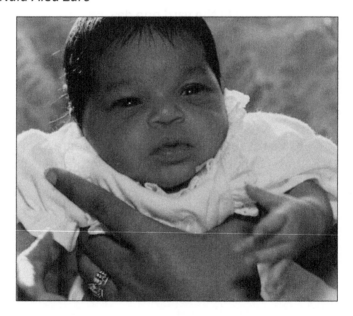

There is the saying, "Time heals all wounds." Some people say it very tritely. Following Kayla's accident and eventual death, it was in no way helpful to me. Yes, time has marched on, and I continue to heal as I will always be in the process of healing until we are reunited, but at that moment, I did not want to think of moving on. My initial thought equated healing to forgetting precious memories or not loving Kayla enough because how can a loving mother "heal?" How can you think of ever seeing any good in the future when a part of you has suddenly and irreversibly been taken away? However, I am now able to find some good in every day because in spite of my troubles, joy has continued to visit me many times over. Flowers, a warm breeze, rain, being able to rest, having peace, my two children, being able to give to others, and even children playing proves that the future can be brighter. Thank you, Jesus, for allowing me undeniably to internalize the truth of knowing that I know there is One that has control over all things. To the mother who birthed a child she has yet to meet—thank you for allowing me to raise her and give her a name.

I would never begin to tell anyone that I know how you feel. Yes, I, too, lost a child, but I lost my child. I had a different relationship with Kayla than you had with your child. Kayla's father and I had a different relationship with her than parents have with their child. Bereaved parents continue to maintain relationships with our children, but in a different way. I have actually found comfort when I heard the late Elizabeth Edwards say when describing her deceased son Wade, *"I have had to learn to parent a memory."* We continue to "parent" as we protect our children's memory and legacy until we are reunited.

People have told me both how strong I was and am which may be true. When I was first told how strong I was, I immediately thought, *"Weak was working for me..."* I may not agree with or understand God's plan, but I trust Him fully. I am well aware that Haven would not have been placed with me if Kayla had lived and I thank Him that I was not in a position to choose. "Kayla's Village" most likely would not have been visualized if Kayla had not died. My life surely would have been different as I continually strive to grow in obedience. Through my testimony, God has worked through me to touch the lives of others exponentially. Kayla has had an impact in her five months of life which was her life expectancy. In no way do I feel that her life was cut short because she accomplished what she was born to do. The ongoing task is to incorporate the loss of my child into my life. Hard?

> *When Jesus returns, I do not want Him to find that I have left some work undone.*

ABSOLUTELY! Yet, doable with the mercy and grace of God which are new every morning? ABSOLUTELY!

My heart was filled with joy as I realized what God was showing me: that even though we die in this human life, we are reborn like butterflies to an infinitely more beautiful state. Our bodies simply encase this beauty. Our souls are set free upon death to the wonder of heaven—if we simply believe in the Lord Jesus Christ and His promise of life everlasting. God will help you through all things whether it is the death of a child, a divorce, multiple job changes, the adoption process, etc.

I Needed The Quiet
author unknown

I needed the quiet, so He drew me aside
Into the shadows where we could confide,
Away from the bustle where all the day long
I hurried and worried when active and strong.
I needed the quiet tho' at first I rebelled—
But gently, so gently, my cross He upheld
And whispered so sweetly of spiritual things.
Tho' weakened in body, my spirit took wings
To heights never dreamed of when active and gay,
He loved me so greatly, He drew me away.
I needed the quiet. No prison my bed,
But a beautiful valley of blessings instead.
A place to grow richer in Jesus to hide.
I needed the quiet, so He drew me aside.

WE WALKED TOGETHER
author unknown

We walked together, you and I,
A mother and her daughter
We had hopes and dreams for tomorrow,
But tomorrow didn't come.
We walked together, you and I,
We talked, we laughed, we loved,
We shared so many happy times
And for that, I thank God above.
We walked together, you and I,
But only for a short time.
For all too soon it ended
Leaving broken hearts behind.
And even though I miss you,
More than words can say,
I thank God that I got to walk with you
Every moment of each day...

We Do Not Need a Special Day
by Connie Dyer

We do not need a special day to bring you to our minds
The days we do not think of you are very hard to find

Each morning when we awake we know that you are gone
And no one knows the heartache as we try to carry on

Our hearts still ache with sadness and secret tears still flow
What it meant to lose you no one will ever know

Our thoughts are always with you, your place no one can fill
In life we loved you dearly in death we love you still

There will always be heartache and often a silent tear
But always a precious memory of the days when you were here

If tears could build a staircase and heartaches make a lane
We'd walk the path to heaven and bring you home again

We hold you close within our hearts and there you will remain
To walk with us throughout our lives until we meet again

Our family chain is broken now and nothing seems the same
But as God calls us one by one the chain will link again

ABOUT THE AUTHOR

Tonya M. Logan became a clinical social worker in May 1991.
Since that time, she has worked in the field of D.C. and Maryland
child welfare with children and families. The positions Tonya has
held over the years are as case manager, adoption worker, clinical
director, foster parent coordinator, recruiter, and founder of a
non-profit organization. As a case manager, she was responsible
for developing and managing the case plans of foster children and
their birth parents as the birth parents worked toward reunifying
with their children. Often, Tonya was required to collaborate with
schools, therapists, pediatricians, and D.C. Superior Court. When she
worked in the area of adoptions, she worked with birth mothers who
were pregnant or had newly delivered their infant. Tonya would help
the birth mother determine whether she had what was required to
raise her child to adulthood. If the birth mother decided to indeed
make an adoption plan for her child, Tonya would help to facilitate
that plan which included contacting the birth father to see if he also
wanted to make an adoption plan or instead raise the infant himself.
When she worked as a clinical director, she would make all attempts
to strengthen and stabilize the birth family so that children need
not enter the foster care system. If children did enter foster care,
Tonya would make referrals so that the situation could be investigated appropriately. She now recruits and licenses foster parents
for treatment teenagers. It is a challenging job, but one Tonya finds
very rewarding and satisfying as she assists in keeping children safe
and finding permanency. Previously, she was a case manager for
an organization that works with the elderly and disabled who are

able to remain in their homes. Tonya helped to ensure that all of their needs were met, that they were being treated with dignity and respect, and that there was no lapse in service.

Tonya has always worked as a contract worker with a variety of agencies and thus learned of common themes and needs. All foster parents are required to obtain a certain number of training hours annually. In July 2007, Tonya began an organization not only to assist foster parents in obtaining their required training hours, but also to provide support and appreciation to them as well as adoptive parents and social service professionals. She named the organization Kayla's Village in honor and memory of her first born daughter.

When asked how she became interested in social work, Tonya stated, *"Honestly, the Lord chose the field of social work for me."* Her undergraduate degree was in psychology and upon graduation, she was not certain as to what she wanted to do. Tonya worked in retail for one year before obtaining her master's degree. She talked to many people who stated that a master's degree in social work afforded the recipient a great deal of flexibility. After doing her internship with those managing mental health issues as well as those who visited an adolescent clinic, Tonya interviewed with several foster care agencies as she was desperately in need of a job. Her plan was to explore working with another population later. After over twenty years in this field, Tonya cannot image doing anything else! God knows best...

There are several rewarding encounters that Tonya has experienced over the years as a social worker. She is reminded of one of her earliest clients who entered the foster care system when she was three years old and Tonya began working with her when she was eleven. Regardless of why children enter the foster care system, they usually idealize their parents and want to return to them. Tonya did not believe the birth mother was a threat to her daughter, but she also did not believe the birth mother would be able to commit to addressing the needs of her daughter. The child was adamant about wanting to experience living with her mother. During one summer, Tonya arranged for the child to spend weekdays with her birth mother and return to her foster home on the weekends. Once the summer ended, the child was clear that she wanted to maintain a relationship with her birth mother, but acknowledged that she would be afforded more stability with her foster mother. Tonya felt good about her decision to allow the child to come to the same conclusion she had without her feeling that she was being "taken" from her birth mother.

In another situation, there were two sisters who had also been in the foster care system for many years. They had experienced many placement disruptions due to the behavior of one of the sisters. The birth mother's parental rights had been terminated by the court. Over the years, the birth mother had worked diligently to improve her life. No adoptive placement was identified for the girls jointly. The birth mother was able to address the individual needs of her daughters. After a great deal of consultation, it was agreed that the daughters would be returned to the birth mother. In order for this to occur, however, the birth mother had to adopt her children as she was no longer legally related to them. Once the adoptions were finalized, the birth mother sent Tonya a card – which she continues to cherish – as she was one who believed in her and helped her to achieve her goal of being the parent she knew she could always be to her daughters.

There are many traits Tonya believes are critical to being an effective social worker and she acknowledges that she does not possess all of them all of the time. She thinks it is necessary to be efficient, strengths-based, compassionate, open, honest, willing to seek help, and willing to admit and learn from mistakes. It is necessary to be a doer and not one who expects someone else to do something. An effective social worker is productive, personable, direct, and able to connect with others which can be accomplished via networking. Tonya believes she does exude the majority of these qualities the majority of the time. Over the years, she has realized that she cannot help everyone and that *"I was not hired to make friends."* Tonya is much more comfortable in her ability to confront and discuss difficult issues without being overly concerned about what others think of her as long as she knows she is doing her very best. She has been blessed to have maintained many friendships in this field throughout the years although several no longer work at the same organization. If someone were asked to describe Tonya as a social worker, she would hope they would say Tonya can be trusted, respects confidentiality, is aware of both personal and professional boundaries, is a team player, and actively advocates for herself. When unclear as to what to do, she makes every effort to allow God to direct her so she can be the best social worker, parent, and person she can be. Tonya has many scriptures that she reflects upon, but a few of her favorites are:

Luke 1:45
"Blessed is she who has believed that the Lord would fulfill his promises to her!"

Jeremiah 29:11
"For I know the plans I have for you," declares the LORD, "plans to prosper you   and   not to harm you, plans to give you hope and a future."

Philippians 4:13
"I can do all things through Christ which strengtheneth me."

The field of social work is often seen as thankless and underpaid. Tonya would like social work to be seen truly as a helping profession rather than as a profession which "takes people's children." Social workers are sometimes seen as the "enemy" to be feared and who are afforded little respect. Some have stated that they do not see why social workers are not volunteers and feel that if someone pays to have an adoption home study completed, in reality they are "paying for a child." Few recognize that fees go toward paying for a service that would otherwise not be available.

In the future, Tonya wishes that when budget cuts are made, those making the cuts would understand that future generations are in reality the ones to suffer if needs are not addressed today. Hurting, vulnerable people are real and not simply names and numbers on some printout. The effect of decisions made today "trickle down" to those who may not be considered. Social workers do a great job of advocating for others, but do not always take good care of or advocate adequately for themselves. During his initial presidential campaign, Barack Obama said, "Yes, we can!" Tonya believes, "Yes, we must!"

Tonya resides in Maryland with her two children, Haven and Christian, as well as her dog, Serenity. She can be reached via kaylasvillage@aol.com.

Continue to be blessed
and a blessing to others...

The author's children, Haven (age 16) and Christian (age 11).

CPSIA information can be obtained at www.ICGtesting.com
Printed in the USA
BVOW11s2105071213

338446BV00005B/7/P